PEACE
WITHOUT
PROZAC

A Book That Heals

Beyond Self-help to Self-healing

Ken R. Unger

M⊙tivational PRESS

LEADERS IN GLOBAL PUBLISHING

Published by Motivational Press, Inc.
1777 Aurora Road
Melbourne, Florida, 32935
www.MotivationalPress.com

Manufactured in the United States of America.

ISBN: 978-1-62865-468-4

1. Health - Healing – United States. 2. Health - Healing – Canada. I. Unger, Ken. II. Title.

CONTENTS

OBLIGATORY LEGAL NOTICE

ACKNOWLEDGEMENTS

B ESIDES FAMILY AND FRIENDS, there are so many people to thank for anyone's success. First are the many people who tell me theye love my writing.Dan Copan, Dave Hummer and others in the Transformational Healing Community in Cleveland mean the world to me.

Then of course there is the long list of people who have been my treasured clients and retreat and seminar attendees since 1979. Without you I could not have learned all I know about healing brokenness. The spiritual mentorship of people like Warren Campbell, Cecile Osborne, and Robert Johnson has taught me so much.

Then there are the people at Faith at Work. They got me started on my retreat journey in the late 70's. Without them I would have missed God's purpose for my life. Thank you all. I am indebted to you in so many ways.

Finally, I'd also like to thank Justin Sachs and his great team at Motivational Press. They are experts who really care about their authors.

ABOUT THE AUTHOR

KEN UNGER IS "AMERICA'S SOUL DOCTOR", a true spiritual healer. A former pastor, spiritual psychotherapist, and former professor of counseling, he knows how to heal your broken places.

He has been leading retreats on personal growth and healing all across the United States for over 35 years. Now his solid scriptural wisdom is available to you.

Don't treat the symptoms, heal your pain. When you heal your pain you no longer need aspirin in whatever form you take it. Don't just care for your soul, cure it!

INTRODUCTION

T IME DOES NOT HEAL ALL wounds. It really doesn't heal any. That is an illusion. As time progresses, the perception of pain merely subsides. New experiences displace our harmful ones, driving them deeper into the subconscious, what I call the basement of the soul, where they lurk to ambush, corrupt, sabotage, and undermine us yet again.

Unless our deepest wounds are truly healed, until our core hurts are appropriately resolved, these hidden denizens of emotional darkness can return at the worst possible moments. I know, because it has happened to me. When my anger bubbled to the surface over a slight, lust yet again reared its ugly head.

The hurts that fuel these setbacks may come from many sources, from outright abuse to "mere" neglect. A woman could have been molested, physically abused or emotionally battered, but she also could have had none of those things happen.

She may have lived in a beautiful home and had plenty to eat while being starved for affection. Many bulimics can tell you that sad tale. Perhaps mommy and daddy were so busy working they never had time to play, or read to her, or even say I love you.

I was physically and emotionally wounded during childhood. My father was a rageaholic. He was angry at his life and he often took it out on me. Consequently, my own anger sometimes surfaced at the most inopportune times.

Other people I know have never heard their parents say, "I love you." Neglect is far subtler than abuse, which is exactly what makes it so difficult to deal with. It is equally damaging and harder to see. Denial is a greater temptation for the victims - yes victims - of neglect.

Our wounds don't have to be parental. Siblings, grandparents, aunts and uncles, schoolmates, teachers, preachers and neighbors all could have harmed us. But wherever our hurts come from, they complicate, inhibit, and plunder our lives, sabotaging our well-being, undermining our dreams, and even possibly destroying our health.

Unhealed pain can fuel alcohol abuse, overeating, codependency, work addiction, perfectionism and other compulsions. It can cause our feelings and our bodies to drive us instead of us comfortably using them.

It eventually pollutes the very things we care about most: our loved ones, our work, our friendships - even our health and prosperity. Unhealed emotional pain is the invisible enemy that causes most of our sufferings and failures in life. It has done all that and more to me.

One of my all-time favorite opening sentences in a book was from M. Scott Peck's, *The Road Less Traveled*. He wrote this: "Life is difficult. But once we accept that fact that life is difficult, life becomes much less difficult."

While this is true, life does not have to be as difficult as we make it. Much of life's struggle is fueled by past hurts that cause us to complicate our life. But if our life is to change, we must find the courage to examine it. The unexamined life is, at best, second-rate.

Though some people may want us to think otherwise, our past is extremely important. Who we are today is largely a result of who we were yesterday and how we handled our problems and hurts from yesterday. But there is nothing that has damaged us that can't be undone.

Even better there is gold in our most sinister shadows, silver linings to our most menacing inner clouds. Our worst tragedies, when properly resolved, can make us better instead of bitter, more whole rather than further fractured, happier instead of more miserable.

Doctors will tell you that once some wounds are properly healed they become stronger and more resilient. The same is true for our inner wounds. The very things that weakened us can give us more strength, power, and vitality. There are countless examples of people who overcame unbearable odds to live successful, beautiful lives.

Because I minister to people out of my own experience of finding the healing I so desperately needed, someone once told me, "Your pain, God's gain."

Nothing fulfills me more than helping people find the healing they need. With God's help, you can redeem your suffering as well.

Nothing will help you more than healing the pain that holds you back. It can do more for your future happiness than anything else. I know. For over twenty-five years it has done this for me and for many hundreds of my clients, friends, former parishioners, and those who attended my seminars and retreats.

One caution: if you don't believe in God, this approach won't help you. That's because only God can heal. There's an old adage in medicine that the physician sets the bone but God heals the break. This also pertains to broken hearts. Only God can free us from the stubborn bondage of self-destructive patterns.

Once the Twelve Step recovery community realized this, they helped millions cut free from their devastating compulsions. God can help you, too. In fact, He's your best ally for your healing journey.

THE FAILURES OF PSYCHOLOGY AND PSYCHIATRY

Both secular psychology and psychiatry have disappointed most people who have sought their help because both have abandoned the metaphysical, thus ignoring the unseen spiritual roots of our difficulties.

This is ironic because both disciplines derive their identity from the word psyche, or soul. The soul is defined by the AOL dictionary as "a: the immaterial and spiritual essence in all rational human beings; b: a person's total self; c: the moral, emotional and spiritual nature of human beings".

The second root word in psychiatry is Iatry, from the Greek *iatreia,* the art of healing and treatment. Psychiatry should treat and heal the spiritual, moral and emotional elements of human personality. Sadly, secular psychiatry simply does not know how to do this.

Instead, psychiatry is largely dominated by modern day medicine men, doctors who often depend exclusively on prescription drugs for treatment. Ironically, the root word for witchcraft is *pharmakeia,* from which, obviously, pharmaceuticals and illicit drugs derive their name.

Psychiatrists can mock the potions and methods of witch doctors, but future generations may well determine that medical psychiatry was equally primitive and ineffective. Clients, as often as not, now come to me today for help getting off of prescription drugs.

One man I know has taken prescription drugs for his anxiety for 30 years. He has seen his current psychiatrist for 20 years, and he's still miserable. Sadly, his story is not uncommon.

According to the New York Times, more than 30 million Americans are currently taking antidepressants. Americans also consume a whopping 80 percent of all prescription painkillers. US doctors write 259 million prescriptions for painkillers each year (some of the most addictive legal drugs). Our modern day medicine men enable millions of Americans to get hooked on drugs that they cannot kick.

Over 95 percent, of the "experimental medicines" that the pharmaceutical industry produces, are found to be unsafe and are never approved. Of the remaining 5 percent that are approved, we seldom discover they are deadly until decades later.

Prescription drugs kill approximately 200,000 people in the United States every year. Drug overdoses alone now kill 50,000 a year, eclipsing traffic deaths in the US. Dr. Sanjay Gupta says accidental prescription drug overdose is "the leading cause of acute preventable death for Americans". In the US painkillers kill more Americans than cocaine and heroin. The CDC says 750,000 rush to emergency rooms for adverse reactions to pharmaceuticals. Over 80% of overdoses result from prescription pain killers. God can heal their pain. That's what Peace Without Prozac does.

The recent Surgeon General's landmark report announced that over 21 million Americans were affected by drug and alcohohol addiction in 2015 – roughly as many who suffer from diabetes - yet fewer than ten percent received treatment. Over 27 million misused prescription or illegal drugs and 66 million struggled with binge drinking. Opioid use has reached crisis levels. (For more on better treatment see my Addendum on Soft Intervention.)

If antidepressants help, why are more Americans killing themselves? The suicide rate, for those aged 35-64, increased by 30 percent between 1999 and 2010. The number of Americans that die by suicide is greater than those who die from car accidents every year. A new study showed that over 25% of new psychiatric diagnoses are attributable to marijuana usage. Think of the implications of that. It has been reported that we spent more than 280 billion dollars on prescription drugs during 2013.

Psychology is no better than psychiatry. Though the word means "knowledge of the soul" the work of psychologists has similarly missed the metaphysical mark. Today, psychology largely depends on cognitive work and talk therapy: treatment from the neck up. The problem with this is that we have forgotten 90 percent of what's happened to us. That means that cognitive therapy can only treat 10 percent of our problems.

Drugs fair no better. They merely treat symptoms, never the root source. Worse, they bring their own complications. A simple Internet web search reveals over 100 serious complications from anti-depressants, many of which can be fatal. Many drugs ruin the sex life and most, if not all have a downside, one that the patient is seldom warned about when he or she starts taking them.

The problem with both the cognitive and chemical approaches to treatment is simply this: neither the mind nor body reflects the essence of the soul. No wonder modern man feels so soulless, and recognizes such a deep spiritual void. Neither talking, nor drugs, nor a combi-nation of both can truly heal the soul's deepest pain.

If you are tired of endless, expensive, ineffective therapies and debilitating prescription drugs, only real healing can change your life. If you desire, above all, to discover what made you the way you are and what you can do about it, if you want to know how to permanently improve your life, spiritual healing will work for you.

I must caution you, just reading anything will not make you healthier. That is why so many self-help books let us down. My approach, STEP therapy, goes beyond self-help to sacred self-healing.

Please just remember, this is not just a book, it is a workbook. If you only read it, it will help you a little bit. If you work it, you can find real healing and forever improve the quality of your life. Who wouldn't want that?

Another thing, you will find parts of the book repetitive. This is by design. I see myself as a teacher, as well as, a healer and we learn best by repetition. To achieve true transformation, we must reinforce the lessons that we need to integrate into our lives.

The Bible says this happens "line upon line, line upon line, precept by precept, precept by precept" (Isaiah 28:10). Athletes know that they must program their body through forced repetitions of the best exercises. If we do that with our heart, mind, soul and strength, our whole lives change.

CHAPTER 1

WHY TWELVE STEPS AREN'T ENOUGH

TWELVE STEP GROUPS HAVE FREED millions of people from the disastrous addictions that destroyed their health, their loved ones, and their well-being. Many people owe their very lives to those groups.

But too often, they have not totally solved people's core problems. Breaking bad habits is great, necessary, an excellent start, but it is not nearly enough to make people whole. Unfortunately, as wonderful as they are, twelve steps don't heal everything.

A person may quit drinking but still be a 'dry drunk', manifesting all the addictive compulsive behavior that drove him to alcohol in the first place. Even worse, without further help, he may swap one addiction for another. The food addict can get hooked on shallow religion, the sex addict on destructive relationships, and the junkie on work or sex. *Until their core issues are resolved, their deepest needs met, until his or her most hurtful pains are healed, no one can be truly whole.*

And without growth towards wholeness, none of us will gain all that life has for us or even come close to reaching our human potential.

All addictions to drugs, alcohol, sex, work, religion, rage or food have this in common: at their roots they are caused by unhealed emotional pain. That is why, to become thoroughly healthy, <u>twelve steps just aren't enough!</u>

We need the fourteenth STEP. STEP is Spiritual Therapy for Emotional Pain. We must heal the pain that binds us.

The idea of a true fourteenth step came to me when a woman attended my retreat who had been leading over eat or is anonymous groups for eight years and was still overweight attended my retreat.

In the middle of the retreat, she grasped how the healing she was receiving was changing her life from the inside out. She started to sob. "This is it," she said. "This is the thirteenth step: real healing for emotional pain." (I didn't want to use the term 'thirteenth step' because in Twelve Step circles it refers to an inappropriate relationship with another group member.)

Everywhere today people recognize their need for healing. For lack of it, many corporations are in a severe state of crisis. There is no way for businesses to measure the enormous cost of the dysfunction of their employees.

Food abuse, marital conflict, illicit affairs, theft, inefficiency, and health problems all rob businesses of fortunes. Some estimate the costs at three billion dollars a year. It may in fact be much higher.

Relational problems with customers, bosses, and co-workers, as well as drug, alcohol and sexual dependencies all take their toll. So do frequent illnesses, absenteeism, and the devastating pain of divorce. Embezzlement and other ethical violations as well as many more subtle problems also undermine productivity.

Most businesses today are pleading for help. They find that secular counseling agencies, churches and synagogues are almost powerless to offer them what they need.

New people coming to church can get tremendous spiritual help but unless their deeper issues are resolved they revert to the same problems that made them seek spiritual help in the first place. I know I did and my conversion was as profound as any I have ever heard.

With it, I received a powerful emotional healing. But soon old behavior patterns crept back into my life. Since my conversion, I have battled pornography, alcohol abuse, rage, and stubborn personality quirks that work against my own best interests.

In all likelihood, even if you have given your life to God, you have fought an often losing battle against similar compulsions and disorders. If it weren't for healing I'd received, I shudder to think what I would be like today.

It is no wonder that church staffs are maxed out trying to keep ahead of their counseling load. They frequently tell me that Bible study, prayer meetings and small groups are no longer enough to get their people healthy. In reality, they probably never were.

Fortunately, we live in an age where people are increasingly aware of their need for healing. This is happening at the same time that they are also being sensitized to their need for what is commonly called spirituality.

This is good news because God must be involved for the

deepest needs of people to be met. The psychiatrist quoted years ago in Newsweek was right when he said, "Psychotherapy without God is malpractice."

Any honest doctor admits that he cannot heal, he can only facilitate healing. Only God is in the healing business. Without His healing power, we only end up treating an endless array of sickening symptoms.

The problem is that few people know how to receive the help that God Himself wants to give them. Hardly any know how to apply His healing power to their own deepest needs.

As you do the exercises each week, they will help you uncover and truly heal your core pain. That is why this is the ultimate self-help book. It summarizes key things I have learned from my own healing quest since 1971.

Though I experienced a life changing conversion and powerful spiritual healing, I was still deeply wounded emotionally. I needed more, much more, to become the person I aspired to be. I bet you do, too.

This book explains what I learned in my quest to help others and myself. It's based on over thirty years of ministering to those deep needs in individual counseling, spiritual therapy, and small groups, as well as the healing seminars and growth retreats I've attended and led all over the United States and abroad since 1979.

BAD RELIGION

Our nation has been widely influenced by religion. Recently, an astonishing 87 percent of Americans surveyed by ABC News said they believe that Jesus is God's son.

Over 80 percent believe that the Bible is the most important book in history. The importance of religion can't be ignored. Good religion, true religion, can be part of the solution. Bad religion is a part of the problem.

The Pharisees, strict religious leaders in Jesus' day, tried hard to discredit the work Christ did to deliver people from the power of the evil one [1]. Jesus posed an enormous threat to them. His healing power exposed the impotency of their hollow religion and won over the hearts and minds of the masses that flocked to Him.

In a vain attempt to undermine Him, the Pharisees accused Jesus of doing the work of Satan. They eventually had Him killed.

Today some well-meaning but misinformed religious leaders still believe that healing isn't necessary. When I started sharing with groups I spoke to about the way in which God was healing people at my retreats, I apparently posed a threat to some pastors.

I was soon released from my position as chairman of the Department of Counseling at a Bible college. Certain preachers spoke against my healing ministry.

Some still preach against it, and sadly, few churches have any ministry in place to heal the hurting in their midst. Though they give lip service to healing, some go so far as to label demonic any attempt to use spiritual gifts to heal the hurting. Most merely offer up feeble prayers for God to "guide the doctor's hands." Many simply make referrals to secular therapists.

When people accused Jesus of doing the devil's work, He called this "blasphemy against the Holy Spirit." He said that this level of deception was the only unforgivable sin. I think He was telling us that those who were so far lost that they thought that the work of the Holy Spirit was the work of the devil were too blinded, too confused to ever be redeemed.

Though few Christians realize it, deep, profound healing was so central to Jesus' mission on earth it became a part of His very name.

Throughout the Bible, names describe a person's calling. They define that person and his or her destiny. In the case of Jesus Christ, what makes this so extraordinary is that few have considered the amazing implications of His name for their lives. We refer to His holy name, we call it His wonderful name, but we don't appreciate what His name really means or all the blessings it contains for us.

Christ is not Jesus' last name; it has a meaning, Messiah, or Anointed One. Anointing is a powerful image. People were anointed on the head with oil to symbolize the way in which they were endowed with divine power - power from above - for their mission in life. Anointing was evidence that a person's work was too hard unless he had God's help.

Even people who realize that Christ means Anointed One seldom comprehend the implications. They think that because kings, prophets, and priests were anointed and Jesus was all of those, then that must be what Christ refers to. In fact, the meaning is far better than that.

In Luke 4:18, Jesus gave what I call His inaugural address. In His very first public speech, He quoted a wonderful passage from Isaiah 61. As Jesus thus defined the purpose of His ministry, He said the reason He was anointed was to heal the brokenhearted, liberate the wounded, set the captives free, proclaim good news to the poor, recovery of sight to the blind, and to preach the acceptable year of the Lord (when they would be released from all their debts and all that was theirs was restored to them) [2].

He understood better than anyone that healing the hurts of individuals is essential if our world is ever going to get better. Without such healing, people could not hope to obey His mandate to love.

Though few people realize it, the very name of Jesus' reflects this. Properly understood it contains some of the greatest blessings we could ever desire. Jesus name was given to him because He would save us from our sins [3].

If we understand sin as the thing that keeps us from radiant glorious living, then this is very good news. But there's more. Jesus is the New Testament name for Joshua. Joshua was the man who led God's people into the Promised Land, a land overflowing with all the abundance and prosperity God's people could ever want.

Yet, in order for the Jews to receive such a wonderful blessing, Joshua had to help them conquer the giants and fierce enemies that occupied that land. Before he died he did exactly that, conquering thirty one other nations without suffering a single defeat.

What does that have to do with us? In the New Testament we learn that our personal Promised Land is the Kingdom of God, a reality that offers us not only material prosperity, but the inner blissful qualities that fulfill the deepest longings of our heart.

That's why Jesus was obsessed with sharing the good news of God's kingdom. This was the only gospel he shared, mentioning it over one hundred and fifty times.

Yet, we too have an adversary that would rob us of our

rightful inheritance as God's beloved children, the inner giants that keep us from enjoying the wonderful blessings of that inheritance, blessings that include peace, prosperity, well-being, joy, love, and a profoundly fulfilling life. Our inner giants are our sins, and contrary to the religious beliefs that many of us have been taught, repentance alone is not enough to overcome these stubborn, powerful inner adversaries. The Apostle Paul told us that sin is lodged within us, and it keeps us from doing and being what we want to do and be [4]. More importantly, our sins are directly related to our wounds [5].

This is precisely why Jesus the Christ was anointed to heal our brokenness. Once our deep emotional wounds are healed, we no longer need the self medicating anesthesia of "sin," and the way it erodes our happiness from the inside out.

We can truly live as free spiritual people. We can better enjoy the blessings of God's kingdom in the present as well as in the world to come. I can tell you this, the more healing I have received, the more whole I have become. With that expanding wholeness I have been able to more fully enjoy the "glorious liberty of God's children," daily experiencing all the blessings inherent in true spirituality.

This includes, but is not limited to, the delicious spiritual fruits of love, joy, peace, patience, and the various virtues that make my life continuously better.

HOW TO GET THE MOST FROM THIS BOOK

Please resist the temptation to race through this book and merely read it. Work it, and it will work for you. By that I mean, spend time with it. You may want to read and meditate upon the footnoted passages listed for your consideration.

Note what they say to you personally. I would even go so far as to say that you shouldn't work through a chapter a day, maybe not even a chapter every couple of days, though that would be easy to do if you approach this book as merely an intellectual exercise.

If you live with this book at the pace of a chapter a week, it will yield wonderful insights for you. It will help you find the healing you need.

It is also important that you answer the questions and do the exercises earnestly. Do that when you are alone and uninterrupted. If you do not remember or are unsure how to answer a journaling question, sit with it for a few days. Ask the Lord to show you how to answer it.

Then let the questions and the insights they foster bubble to the surface. Sometimes it takes days to answer them because the true answer may be buried deep within the subconscious and need time to fight its way to the surface.

Each time you do this, you will be taking the necessary STEP, and you will begin to receive the appropriate reward: Spiritual Therapy for Emotional Pain.

It will then lead you to the highest power of healing for the wounds that have bound you and held you back. Let me offer another caution.

Because God is essential for healing and our whole culture has been more influenced by the Bible than by any other book, I have used Biblical references liberally. If you do not believe in the Bible, I can understand and appreciate that.

I was raised in a very liberal church where I was taught to

disbelieve it. For a while, I was even an atheist, but that was because I did not really understand the profound, practical wisdom of the Bible.

But even if you do not believe all of it is literally true, please reflect on its simple, yet profound, spiritual truths. They operate on many deep levels in our life. All I ask is that you consider it, as you might any book of great wisdom, as perhaps having some validity for you.

If it is true, it will reveal itself as such. May God, however you understand Him, richly bless and encourage your heroic healing journey.

SCRIPTURE TO MEDITATE ON THIS WEEK:

"The Spirit of the Lord is upon me because He has anointed me to preach the gospel to the poor, He has sent me to heal the broken-hearted, to preach deliverance to the captives, and recovery of sight to the blind, To set at liberty those who are oppressed, To preach the acceptable year of the Lord." (Luke 4:18-20)

In what way are you poor? _____

Brokenhearted? _____

Captive? _____

Blind? _____

Oppressed? _____

What good news would you like to ask the Lord to share with you in these areas?

_____

_____

_____

_____

_____

FOOTNOTES:

[1] Matthew 12:22-37

[2] Luke 4:18-20

[3] Matthew 1:21

[4] Romans 7:15-23

[5] Jeremiah 30:14-15

Read Luke 4:18-20, and Isaiah 61:1-7 from which it was taken. Write down what it means to you. What do you hope these promises will do for you when they are fulfilled?

_____

_____

_____

_____

_____

JOURNALING QUESTIONS:

1. Have you ever been in a twelve-step group, Bible study, or other small personal growth, therapy or healing group? If so, how did it help?

_____

_____

_____

_____

_____

2. What limitations did you see in the groups you were in?

_____

_____

_____

_____

3. What, if anything, do you wish the groups could have done for you but didn't?

_____

_____

_____

_____

_____

4. If you could have anything you want happen to you because of completing this workbook, what would it be? (Be
specific.)

_____

_____

_____

_____

_____

5. Ask God, however you envision Him, to do that very thing.
Write it down and date it.

_____

_____

_____

_____

_____

CHAPTER 2

SOME PEOPLE DON'T WANT YOU HEALED

HEALING EMOTIONAL PAIN HAS become controversial in some circles. This is especially true for some conservative religious groups. Some actually feel that healing is unnecessary.

These people maintain that conversion is enough, that a person does not need anything else. They say that spiritual rebirth totally fulfills Christ's mission to heal the brokenhearted.

To be sure, the rebirth is a wonderful new beginning, a life-changing encounter with the living God, but it's just the beginning. We must progress far beyond that, and much of our progress hinges on becoming more whole. Jesus intended for conversion to be a new beginning, not an end.

The root word for salvation is rich with this understanding. Salvation literally means an on-going growth towards wholeness, not just an ethereal Heavenly reward. Jesus did not just come to earth to offer us free fire insurance, He came to give us an abundant life.

Rebirth is essential to the Christian message. Being reborn

makes a person new, connecting our spirit with the Spirit of the living God and affording us a chance to start a whole new life. But what newborn baby is fully mature?

If conversion were all we needed, the Bible would not have told us that God gave gifted leaders to the Church to help us become what we're meant to be. He clearly gave pastors, teachers, apostles and prophets to the Church [1]. He also gave us gifts of healings (note the plural in ICor.12:9) and of miracles [2].

These leadership gifts were given to the Church, not the outside world. Why would He give us these things if they weren't necessary?

As we will see, He predicted that we would need healing gifts in a special new way at the end of time, and it is entirely possible we are living at the very end of time. That may explain why many people have been receiving knowledge about healing that others did not understand before.

The God of the Bible promised to dispense such knowledge precisely as Jeremiah predicted, in Jeremiah 30 when God said He would heal the pain of His people. Jeremiah ended that chapter by saying, "In the latter days you will understand this" [3].

Others say that the emphasis on inner healing is too introspective, and that can be a danger. Some people in the healing ministry act as if life is just one endless emotional archaeological dig. Certainly, God never intended that. Excessive introspection is no healthier than constantly ignoring your shortcomings. But there is a time for everything. The Bible clearly indicates that before a person takes communion, what Catholics call the Eucharist, we should examine ourselves and confess our sins.

Healing is like that. You would not want to be hooked up to an MRI machine all the time, but when you are ill, it is necessary to diagnose the disease. That is what the introspection of healing ministry is all about.

Unless we occasionally take stock of our lives we can never get better and everything that doesn't get better usually gets worse. The unexamined life can come unraveled.

As you do the journaling and other things suggested in this book you will see and identify the things that are responsible for your failures, hurts, and frustrations. This will lead you into the things you must see, understand, and experience to be healed of your pain.

This is not needless introspection. It is necessary self-examination, and you and your world will become better if you learn to do this well.

Other religious people may object that some of the techniques we use are not in the Bible, but neither is a Buick, a dentist's drill, or an X-ray machine.

Who would insist that we only use donkeys for travel or forsake modern medicine? As long as what we do to heal our pain is not contrary to responsible Biblical teaching; we can be assured of God's blessing and protection

Finally, many well-meaning pastors and religious counselors have only two pills in their spiritual medicine cabinet. They tend to use one or the other in every situation.

What I mean is that they often act as if there are only two things necessary in any situation. What are those two pills? Many seem to believe that all the problems we have can be solved through either repentance or forgiveness. They seem to think that if you have done something wrong, all you need to do is repent and you will be fine.

If someone has wronged you, they imply that all you need to do is forgive them and again you will be fine. Repentance and forgiveness are important, but neither are panaceas.

Sins, whether those we commit or those committed against us, damage us. No one has escaped life unscathed. To become whole, we all require healing.

Guilt is too often the motivator of choice for much preaching and religious counseling. I was shocked when I resigned from my church and moved to California.

After 23 years in pastoral ministry I looked forward to selecting a church to attend. I soon found that most pastors talk way too long and almost always use guilt as the primary motivator in their sermons.

Ironically, Jesus seldom used guilt to motivate sincere seekers. Instead, he expressed compassion and appealed to their understanding. His strictest condemnation was reserved for religious leaders whom He said, "Heaped burdens upon men's shoulders too grievous to be born," and were unwilling to help them carry their load. Mostly these burdens involved judgment, guilt, and condemnation.

Most people, who are bound by destructive behaviors, already feel guilty enough. They have repented countless times but nothing ever changed. Similarly, most who were wronged have diligently tried to forgive, but have never been freed of their resentment.

That is because underlying most sins, both those we have committed and those committed against us, are unhealed emotional wounds.

Time and again I have seen tremendous release and powerful victory once those underlying emotional hurts are healed. People bound by sin finally find it possible to repent once their pain is healed. After all, only God can grant repentance, [4] but it's easy to seek repentance once our pain is healed and we no longer need sin's soothing anesthetic.

Those who are bound up in resentment are released into true forgiveness once the hurt they received has been redeemed. Then they can actually see their pain work to their benefit. This is why Jesus launched His earthly mission by stressing the necessity of healing the broken-hearted, liberating those who were bruised, and releasing the captives [5].

However, not all objections to healing come from the religious community. Doctors tell many people today that their problems have chemical or genetic roots. This is modern medicine's scapegoat for the ills they can neither heal nor understand.

While some mentally ill people have a different chemical makeup, drugs alone won't solve all their problems. Chemical imbalances offer no proof that some people are born with certain mental inclinations.

It is entirely feasible that the different chemical makeup of a schizophrenic is not congenital, but may instead be the result of unhealed emotional pain. This pain may have even been suffered in the womb, ironically lending apparent credence to the opinion that a person is indeed born that way.

In reality, drugs have a limited role in the healing process. They can be used to stabilize a person or restore them to functionality so that they can receive the healing and counseling they need, but beyond that they can often become part of the problem.

A person should not stop taking their prescriptions unless their doctor approves it and they truly believe, without any doubt, that they are no longer necessary. (Even then they should be carefully tapered off of the drugs in consultation with their doctor.) But most, and perhaps all, drugs merely treat symptoms.

They seldom, if ever, heal anything. In many cases, drugs can block the powerful feelings that need to surface and be resolved through proper healing ministry and counseling.

Through spiritual healing, we have achieved exceptional results by helping people get to the root cause of their problems. Often this affects both physical symptoms and their psychological and emotional causes. A friend's experience offers a case in point.

She called one day and asked if I could see her right away. Her migraines were driving her up a wall. The new pills her doctor had prescribed for her, which cost 60 dollars a piece, hardly even dented her pain.

In a short time we found the onset of her problem. I simply asked her when her migraines started. She told me they began ten years earlier. I asked what was happening in her life at that time and lights went on immediately.

She had suffered a terrible emotional trauma at the hands of a loved one. She dealt with the superficial issues and had dutifully tried to forgive the person who had wronged her but in doing so, she suppressed all the pain involved.

Before we talked about it she never realized that this was exactly when her migraines started. Using the simple techniques I will explain later, I ministered so much healing to her that she soon said she felt better than she had in ten years.

Some people are highly suspicious of medical cures and with good reason. A former counseling client recently said, "Ken, I need your advice. While my husband and I were coming to one of your counselors things got much better. Then my husband got a new job and his health coverage allowed us to see a free licensed therapist. The problem is they gave our son a diagnosis that he now uses to excuse himself from dealing with his issues. They also prescribed medication to control his symptoms and he's now worse than ever."

This is not an isolated complaint. While there are some competent therapists who help people truly work towards resolving their core issues, too many depend on prescription drugs alone to treat their patient's problems.

The book *Toxic Psychiatry* revealed the connections between the drug companies and therapists that served both industries very well, but did little or nothing to truly help the patients.

Like modern medicine men, many psychiatrists are little more than legalized pushers, endlessly prescribing expensive and debilitating drugs, which never have the power to heal and make people whole.

Let me repeat, drugs treat symptoms. I know of no psychotherapeutic drug that heals anything. However, even some Christian counselors use medicine in this way, assuming that a person must forever depend on drugs that merely mask or suppress their symptoms.

A famous Christian therapist teaches that for some people, drugs are essential for the rest of their lives. He totally neglects the great news that the Lord promised to heal all our diseases [6}, body, soul, and spirit [7]. And God has never promised something He can't deliver.

Again, I would never tell someone to stop taking their prescriptions until and unless they had absolute confidence that they were unnecessary. Yet, all too often, drugs are seen as an end in themselves.

Years ago, I had a discussion with a Manhattan psychiatrist who ran a methadone clinic. I innocently asked him how many people in his program became healed.

He looked at me as if I were from another planet. "Healed?" he said. "What do you mean by healed?"

"You know, healed," I replied. "Healthy enough to never again need drugs."

I'll never forget his response. "No one gets healed," he said. "If we're fortunate, we help 15 percent a little bit, but no one gets healed."

For many hours, we discussed the work I do in healing people through God's power. He never knew such a thing was possible. He openly admitted to me that shortly after being licensed to practice psychotherapy, he realized so much of it was quackery that he almost changed professions, but he had too much invested in his education.

Instead he decided to run the methadone clinic. Similarly, many pastors and Christian counselors don't realize the impotency of prescription solutions. Sadly, most of them also refer parishioners to medical psychiatrists and secular psychologists.

I know the limited effectiveness of drugs first hand. When I had a drug induced psychotic episode in college, it was obvious my doctors did not have a clue what to do for me. The only thing they had to offer was prescription drugs.

I soon became so addicted to them that they eventually pushed me to the very brink of suicide. If the Lord had not healed me I would be dead today, probably by my own hand.

Even if a person is born with chemical differences these could have developed in the womb, or even before. There is such a thing as generational sin that can affect us in terrible ways, from three to four generations back, [8] and there are still no drugs that can heal it.

Only God can do that. The only way any medicines can truly help is if they correct the underlying imbalance, but I'll share more on that later.

Let me repeat, the Lord promised to heal all our diseases. I believe our energies are much better spent learning about healing and working towards it than constantly medicating ourselves.

A man once came to me because his pastor said I might know of a Christian psychiatrist. He had suffered two psychotic episodes and had been taking prescription psychotropic drugs for over 18 years.

I told him I did not know of any doctor like he wanted. He asked what I did and I told him I believed in healing and helped people work towards it. He asked if I would see him as a client and I consented.

Before our first session, he decided he did not want to take any more drugs. I gave him this book and instructed him in how to use it. After two sessions, he stopped taking the drugs for the first time in 18 years.

Soon, he got a new job and thanked me profusely for the help he'd received. I never even did any hands on healing work with him! I merely counseled him twice, gave him the book, and God did the rest. That is why our approach has gotten results where medicine, psychiatry, religion, and psychology have not. God is the unseen ally to all our healing work.

One man came to me on the brink of suicide. He had been to four different counselors, none of whom could help him. After a few months and just a handful of sessions, he saw where his pain came from and how to heal it. Though he was dyslexic, he went back to school, graduated with honors, and made a whole new career for himself.

Another woman, a former nun, came to me after years of seeing secular therapists. She too, was on the brink of suicide. She had paid thousands of dollars to psychologists, and owed her current doctor over 10,000 dollars. After three sessions, total cost was under 600 dollars, and she was well enough to no longer need my help.

The truth is that God did not make some people crazy. Insanity is bound up in the heart of every person [9]. We could all come unglued. The good news is that if we do, He can even heal us of that.

The world needs God's healing power more than ever. It is desperately hungry for it, and God has not only promised it but provided it for us.

The sooner we learn how to appropriate it, the sooner His Kingdom can come to earth and make it more heavenly. If that healing is "from the devil", as some religious people claim, Satan is awfully confused.

God has given healing gifts to His Church, but most of them lie unopened beneath the celestial Christmas tree, and that needs to change. The Church should be a hospital for sinners, not a museum for saints; a sinner's anonymous rather than a saint's autonomous. The sooner it becomes that, the better.

Again, to recap, the very name Christ means anointed one. Jesus Himself said He was anointed to heal the broken hearted and set the captives free. Healing is often necessary before we can be truly free.

Walking in freedom is essential if we are to find all the blessings and the abundant life He intends for us. It's the very essence of the abundant kingdom living He intends for us.

Today, He wants to use His people, the Church, to do that vital healing work. With all the pain and dysfunction in the world around us it's high time we followed His lead in this crucial, powerful, and exciting work.

SCRIPTURE TO MEDITATE ON THIS WEEK:

"'For I will restore you to health and heal you of your wounds,' says the Lord...'In the latter days you will under-stand this.'" (Jeremiah 30:17, 24)

What wounds do you want Him to heal for you?_____

_____

FOOTNOTES:

These scriptures were used in this chapter. It will help you to take a separate sheet of paper, look each one up, and write out what they mean to you. I suggest you do this after reading each chapter.

_____

[1] Ephesians 4:11-13

[2] I Corinthians 12:7-11

[3] Jeremiah 30:24

[4] II Timothy 2:25

[5] Luke 4:18-20

[6] Psalm 103:3

[7] Thessalonians 5:23 (The word sanctify, or make holy, is related to the word make whole or complete. It relates powerfully to healing.)

[8] Exodus 20:5-6 (Right in the middle of the Ten Commandments the Lord warns us of the powerful potential which generational sin has to harm us. He also gives us the clues we need to free us from its grip, which I will discuss later.)

[9] Ecclesiastes 9:3

JOURNALING QUESTIONS:

1. What have you heard of the objections to healing ministry presented in this chapter?

_____

_____

_____

_____

_____

2. How do you feel about them?

_____

_____

_____

_____

_____

3. What areas of your life would you like to see healed?

_____

_____

_____

_____

_____

4. What do you believe that would do for you?

_____

_____

_____

_____

_____

CHAPTER 3

DON'T JUST TREAT THE SYMPTOMS, HEAL THE PAIN

ONCE AGAIN, TIME DOES NOT heal all wounds. In reality it does not heal any. It is merely an illusion that dulls our pain, a sugarcoated placebo that doesn't hurt but also doesn't truly heal. Untreated, unresolved hurts neither go away nor are harmless.

Whether we remember them or not, whether we feel them or are numb to their ongoing impact, the hurts we have failed to heal make their presence known in many powerful but subtle ways. Unhealed pain exacts its relentless revenge on all the important areas of our lives.

Compulsions like the abuse of drugs, alcohol, food, work addiction, relational problems, nagging anxiety, and depression, as well as repeated failure, self-sabotage, or other destructive means can all destroy our well-being.

We have all tried many things to deal with our pain. How many books have we bought and not finished? How many talks have we heard and pills have we taken that didn't truly work? How many counselors have we consulted, and promising methods attempted, that may have helped for a little while but never effectuated lasting change?

A dear friend of mine went to a psychiatrist twice a week for over three years, investing over 75,000 dollars in today's money in therapy. He told me that in one ten-minute session at one of our Spiritual Healing Retreats he learned the real source of the problem for which he had sought treatment.

When he worked with the insight he gained, he saw tremendous results in his family, work, and all other important relationships. In fact, within a couple of months he consummated a business deal that had a net profit of over five million dollars. He said that without the insights he had gained from that one ten-minute session, it would have been impossible.

In truth, most of the books, counselors, and therapies we try also merely treat the symptoms. Few, if any, ever touch the roots of our problems. The reasons for this are simple.

Knowing why you have a problem does not make it go away. Knowing what to do doesn't somehow render you instantly capable of doing it.

Treating emotional problems with either drugs or mere talk doesn't resolve the core issues. Emotional problems require emotional solutions. Until our unhealed pain is properly resolved, we may become temporarily better, or change things a little bit, but real life-changing trans-formation will elude us.

Without true healing, the abundant life for which we all yearn will remain forever beyond our frail grasp. The love, joy, peace, happiness, and fulfillment which we desire will remain unattainable.

While the diagnosis is simple, the prescription is not. It is as complicated as each individual person. This is why the endless parade of books, therapists, treatments, and methods keeps marching through our lives with little long-term effect.

It has taken us our whole lives to complicate things and it will take us a while to sort things out. In fact, that is one of the major reasons we are alive.

In religious language, the process of becoming more whole is known as sanctification. In the vernacular, it's getting your stuff together or something like that. If we do this right, we come to know God and ourselves much better.

We also become the kind of people that we hope to become, and in the process help make the world a better place. At least that is how it is supposed to work. We do not need to wait until after we die to finally become whole.

The healing journey does not have to be a perpetual, gruesome experience. In fact, the journey truly is the destination. When I first heard that, I naively thought it was a hollow phrase, but it isn't.

The healing journey, the one truly heroic quest each of us can make, can actually become quite pleasant. That is because the better we get, the richer and fuller our lives become.

You can't improve yourself without substantially improving your life. In fact, the only way to genuinely improve our lives is to improve ourselves. Once we become fully committed to that process we are well along the way to achieving that abundant life we read about but never quite obtain.

The good news is that there is realistic hope for profound lasting personal growth, development, and glorious change. It's not only possible, but quickly accessible.

When I say we need God's help, I do not mean this in the sense you have traditionally known religion. The word religion is only mentioned three times in the Bible and only once positively. Bad religion got Jesus killed and it can snuff out his life in us as well.

Bad religion, when not in serious denial about our deepest needs, is often suffocating, and at worst counter-productive to the healing journey. Truly, the letter of God's law kills but the spirit gives life [II Corinthians 3:6] yet with the Lord's help, our lives can soon dramatically improve.

He is, after all, the Prince of Peace, the Lord who offers us eternal life, and the only One anointed to heal the broken hearted. No other deity in any great religion ever made such promises or was given such a mission.

The Old Testament predicted that the Son of Righteous-ness will arise with healing in His wings. It states that when that happens we will literally skip about for joy as we more fully experience His incredible gift of abundant life [1].

I have seen people do that at our Healing Retreats and Seminars. I remember praying for a woman at a church service in Washington. I was surprised when the Lord told me to tell her He would touch her with healing and it would make her so happy she would not even be dignified about it.

This charming, gracious older lady looked at me, smiled, removed her high heels, and went skipping and leaping around the sanctuary whooping and hollering for joy. The congregation broke out in amazed, spontaneous applause. How is such joy and freedom possible?

The One who created us, who knew us before we were born [2], knows everything that made us the way we are. He has witnessed every hurt we have ever encountered including the ones we have long since forgotten, the ones we somehow think that time has mysteriously healed. Better yet, he knows everything we need in order to heal our hurts and make us whole.

But the best news is this: He loves us deeply, carrying in His huge heart a profoundly personal affection for each one of us. He is willing and eager to give us everything we need to achieve the greatest wholeness and satisfaction possible in life.

I went to church for many years and didn't ever hear what I am about to tell you. Jesus Himself said He came for this very reason: that we might have an abundant life [3].

As wonderful as Heaven is going to be it is not the only reason Jesus came to earth. Eternal life isn't just pie in the sky when we die, it's pie on the plate. We can have our cake and eat it too.

True faith isn't about denying ourselves and living boring lives so we can get heavenly retirement benefits. Jesus came to earth to help us enjoy this life as well. He came to help us grab the real gusto He has for us.

The best way to do this is by finding and fulfilling our true destiny. He does, after all, have a wonderful purpose for each of us, a calling uniquely designed for the special person He made each of us to be.

And, in my experience, after wasting years of my life "doing my own thing" and studying other philosophies and religions, the one thing that works best is finding and doing God's will. He knows better than I do who I am, and He knows what He has uniquely created me to do.

Nothing has given me greater satisfaction than discovering His grand plan for my life. Further, nothing makes Him happier than seeing His children thriving and doing well in all ways, body, soul, and spirit.

Why would He care about this? Saint Augustine said, "the glory of God is man fully alive," and he's right. Nothing better reflects the goodness and profound wisdom of God than men and women who are full of love, joy, and peace.

Besides, if I want my children happy, healthy, and prosperous, and my own love is imperfect and tainted by self-interest, how much more does God want all good things for each us?

If we are to find and do God's will we must live as truthfully as we can. There is such a thing as what Francis Schaeffer called true Truth. That just means that Truth is ultimately expedient. It's in our best interests to obey it.

As someone wisely said, things are not true because they are in the Bible; they are in the Bible because they are true.

Something is true because it works. That means that when we live according to the Truth it is to our highest advantage. It is the most effective way to accomplish something.

What God is seeking to accomplish on earth is nothing less than a foretaste of Heaven. That is what we ask for in the Lord's Prayer when we pray "Thy Kingdom come, thy will be done, on earth as it is in Heaven."

We are acknowledging that where His will is done, earth becomes Heavenly. And contrary to some bad press it has been getting lately, Heaven is not going to be dull.

It is a splendid place, where love and genuine joy reign supreme, and all suffering and want is permanently abolished. If that is to be modeled on earth, those same things must characterize our daily life.

So, what is the truest way to live? The Bible is very clear on this. Love is the most important thing we are created for [4]. More than anything else, love embodies the lifestyle of His Kingdom.

Love is risky business. We have all been hurt by love. Pain, grief, and suffering inhibit the flow of God's love. That is why He is intensely interested in healing us.

This is precisely why there is so much healing mentioned and demonstrated in the Bible. God heals, not out of some vain egotistical need to show off or to prove that Jesus was the Messiah, but because He is the very essence of Love.

That's why those who claim that healing is not for today are woefully misguided. Who of us, if we saw our loved ones suffer, would not want to heal them? God doesn't heal to prove something, or establish his reputation, He heals because He is Love, and He is the same yesterday, today, and forever [5]. God still heals today. Evidence of this abounds.

Sadly, most seminaries and Bible schools don't teach pastors and ministers how to appropriate God's healing, but it's not God's fault, or even will, that there is so little healing, it's ours.

God's Kingdom is truly the Kingdom of health, wholeness, well-being, and love. Its primary characteristics are righteousness, peace and joy [6]. That is why I say the benefits of His Kingdom begin in this life.

They start within the human heart. His Kingdom is internal as well as eternal. And since the heart, our inner life, is where all the things originate that destroy our well being [7], He's in the business of changing us from the inside out. That is why merely changing our behavior is not enough.

How do I know? Twenty-six centuries ago the Lord promised to heal the pain of His people (Read Jeremiah 30). He then said that in the latter days we would understand this, and for almost thirty years I've been helping others and myself find the healing He promised to give us.

This book is written to show you how to receive the emotional and deep spiritual healing He promised us. And, since I am very much still a work in progress myself, I can make no claims to perfection.

Though I will guarantee you this, if you apply the simple spiritual realities I'm going to share with you it will do more to bless and change your life than any book, pill, or therapy ever could and sooner than you think. Join me on the heroic healing journey. You will not regret it, and you may just be eternally grateful.

Before journaling read each of the scriptures mentioned in the footnotes and jot down what they say to you personally.

SCRIPTURE TO MEDITATE ON THIS WEEK:

"I have come that you may have life, and that you may have it more abundantly." (John 10:10)

FOOTNOTES:

[1] Malachi 4:2

[2] Ephesians 1:4

[3] John 10:10

[4] Romans 13:8

[5] Hebrews 13:8

[6] Romans 14:17

[7] Mark 7:15-23

JOURNALING QUESTIONS:

1. List the most painful experiences you can remember in your life and your approximate age when they happened.

Painful Event – Age – Person Responsible

_____

_____

_____

_____

_____

2. Put a * next to the ones which you feel are unresolved and may contain some unhealed pain.

3. Number these unresolved painful experiences in order of their magnitude. Number the worst one 1, the next 2, etc.

4. Who, if anyone, including you was most responsible for each hurt?

5. What is your relationship like with these people now? Include how you feel about yourself.

_____

_____

_____

_____

_____

6. Which, if any of these people, have you found it hard to forgive? Mark them with an X.

7. Read Matthew 6:14. What would it take for you to forgive them from the heart?

_____

_____

_____

_____

_____

CHAPTER 4

WISDOM FROM THE BEDROCK OF OUR CULTURE

I DO NOT KNOW IF ANY politicians truly care about your pain, but the God of the Bible does. And that is important. I was a psychology major who cracked up in my senior year of college.

In a couple of weeks I went from being a big man on campus with graduate scholarships to study in the best universities around the world, to being so far out of touch with reality that I thought I was Jesus.

There were many reasons for my breakdown, which is the subject of another book, but in my mind the dominant cause was the fact that I had wandered far from the way in which the Lord created us to live.

Believing the dominant cultural myths of our time, I thought that truth was relative, guilt was merely psychological, and I could do whatever I felt like doing and not suffer any consequences.

Boy was I wrong. We are not punished for our sins, we are punished by them. I had to lose my mind, my religion, and almost my life to discover that. After an intense secular quest failed to show me how to get the most out of life, after atheism proved to have no handle on happiness, and after all the state's doctors, social workers, and psychiatrists couldn't put this Humpty Dumpty back together again I finally had to turn to the God of the Bible. He alone could help me find hope of real healing and show me how to have a life worth living again.

Thankfully, my search was not in vain. When I turned my life over to Him, the Lord did for me what my training in psychology could not. He instantly healed my psychosis. I was so much better I thought I would never again need counseling, healing, or therapy, but a few years later I made a startling discovery.

Though at my conversion the Lord had instantly, powerfully, and dramatically healed my schizophrenia, I still was not completely whole. The results of all my years of rebellion against Him left me with a sorry legacy of unhealed hurt and heartbreak.

Even after I became a Christian I suffered more hurt and pain. Call it spiritual friendly fire, but I became a "burned-again" Christian. Perhaps no one can hurt you worse than your Christian brothers and sisters, yet I was learning an invaluable truth:

WHERE SIN ABOUNDS, PAIN ABOUNDS.

I had been a world-class sinner. From my earliest teen years, I had partied hard, used people, and lived a hedonistic, selfish life. Now, though I was truly healed of the psychosis (as was later confirmed by extensive psychological tests), all the accumulated hurts that made me so vulnerable to the sin that almost destroyed me were still unresolved.

Though my mind was healed, I was still emotionally damaged. It would take more than an instant healing to become whole. I also learned that I'd need a lot of help along the way.

In the Old Testament the nation of Israel is analogous to the life of every Christian. Their exodus from Egypt; the land of Sin, and their wilderness trek in search of the Promised Land symbolizes our quest for wholeness.

Like them, we seek to be free from bondage. Like them, we too experience the trials of a howling wilderness in our lives. We also desire a better life, one where abundance replaces subsistence level living, where we can thrive not just survive, living joyfully in peace and prosperity, free from our enemies' torments.

At a deeper level, Biblical truth, like other great religious writings, explores and enlightens our personal pilgrimage. When I realized that my life was not as healthy as I thought, my circumstances were similar to Israel's during Jeremiah's time.

Like Israel, I had forsaken my life in the howling, desert wasteland of sin. Like them, in my quest for a better Way, I had trekked the howling inner wilderness where I was sorely tempted to return to my own personal Egypt; to exchange my freedom for the ease, comfort, and harsh bondage and passing pleasures of sin. Like them, I discovered that the only way around was through the wilderness.

That to get the most out of life I had to "go on in God," to embrace His oft difficult purpose for my life, to live with the Lord as my King. Like them I had tasted the goodness of the Promised Land, the glorious inner Kingdom that resides deep within the heart of every committed believer. Like them, I had become presumptuous, trying to serve God and satisfy my own needs my own way.

Though I was a seminary student and part time pastor, and had spent years in full time ministry, I thought I could keep one foot in God's Kingdom and the other in "the world." I thought I could live for His will and do my will. Much like ancient Israel did in Biblical times.

After their wilderness wanderings, Israel had occupied Palestine. Under Joshua they began to drive out God's enemies, subduing the Promised Land to His rule. At some point, they became complacent and made their peace with the devil.

Somewhere along the way, they stopped driving out the Canaanites and gradually began to embrace their values and lifestyle. They stopped living righteously and trusted that their empty religious rituals would save them. They took God for granted, assuming that since they were Jews, God would never abandon or judge them.

Into that setting, the Lord raised the prophet Jeremiah to warn the people of their wicked ways. His message was simple, if they failed to acknowledge how far they had wandered and return to the Lord He would judge their sin and allow them to go back into bondage. Their enemies would again conquer them.

Jeremiah was not popular. No one likes bad news, especially if it is about them. The people were so intent on silencing him that at one point they dragged him through manure, but he would not be quiet even though they refused to listen to him.

So, just as the Lord said, their enemies conquered them and carried them off to Babylon making them exiles in a foreign land. Their spiritual bondage led to physical bondage. They again became slaves to their enemies. They became indentured servants not only of sin, but also of a conquering foreign power.

A similar thing happened to me. Though I had joyfully served the Lord when I first gave Him my life, I gradually saw that the Lord would not allow me to run my life the way I wanted. I lived as if the Bible said, "The Lord is my butler, I shall not want." The problem is He didn't quite see it that way.

A famous Bible teacher says that when you meet the Lord you meet the first person you can never manipulate. God would not do everything my way. When I saw that, I began to withdraw from Him and take my life back into my own hands.

Along with that came a gradual, subtle, but relentless return to bondage. I was carried back to my own inner Babylonian captivity. My old sins began to overtake me once again. As soon as I stopped delighting in the Lord and taking pleasure in His will, I sought pleasure in the things that the world, the flesh, and the devil offered me instead. As with Israel, it was the beginning of my downfall.

When we shut God out our spirit grows cold and dark, and our bodies cry out for comfort, release, and indulgence. Like the proverbial dog returning to his vomit, I went back to my old ways of meeting my needs, but whenever we feed the flesh first our spirits whither. My capacity for love, joy, and peace soon evaporated.

One thing I know about sin is that it's a promising employer but a lousy paymaster. Sin proffers a fulfillment it can't provide. Why? We are spiritual people and sin only gratifies the flesh. Its temporary satisfactions are limited to the shallowest level of our being.

Therefore, whether our indulgence of choice is food, drink, drugs, sex, self-righteousness, rage, or work, the more we have of our substance or favorite activity the more we crave. There is always a diminishing return.

Each time we illegitimately attempt to satisfy a legitimate need, we need more of that substance or activity to get the desired effect. The more we overindulge our desires the more harmful our sins become.

Before I became a Christian I used to say, "As long as you don't hurt anyone you can do whatever you want." Yet, there's no such thing as a sin that never hurt anyone. At the very least, sin always hurts the sinner. That's why I love the sentiment I read years ago. I believe it came from a man named James Stewart:

God loves broken sinners, but He hates the sin that broke them. God is not against us for our sins, rather He is for us against our sins.

However, like the prodigal son in Jesus' parable, until we experience the consequences of our rebellion we will not want to be freed from the vice of sin.

Prodigal doesn't mean terrible, it just means wasteful. The prodigal son was wasting his inheritance. After all, when he returned to his father's house it was not because he was afraid of where he would spend eternity. Rather he came to his senses and realized that his father's servants had a better life as slaves than he had doing his own thing.

The whole nation of Israel had to come to the same conclusion. They had to stop blaming God and Jeremiah for their problems, and acknowledge that they had caused their own suffering, bondage, and eventual downfall. They had to stop playing the blame game and accept personal responsibility for their unpleasant plight.

We must do the same if we want to be healed. Jeremiah was known as the healing prophet because in Israel's darkest hour he explained to them what had happened, and offered them the hope of healing and restoration.

In the thirtieth chapter of Jeremiah he explained how they got into the mess they were in, and what the Lord would have to do to deliver them. In effect, he told them that they were not bad, just bruised. Their sins had caused them to suffer greatly. By the time they were ready to listen, their wounds were incurable [1].

Although nothing else could help them and their situation was truly hopeless, God Himself promised to heal their pain [2]. He then said something wonderfully mysterious. He told them that in the latter days they would understand what this was all about [3].

I believe we are in those latter days. Again, where sin abounds pain abounds - and I am not sure there has ever been a time or society where sin was more openly celebrated. It is the real reason why so many of us are hurting.

It's why His promise is such very good news. The promise He made through Jeremiah is being fulfilled in our day. It's a promise made to us. The Living God, the One who created Heaven and earth, will truly heal our pain.

SCRIPTURE TO MEDITATE ON THIS WEEK:

"Your affliction is incurable, your wound is very severe. There is no one to plead your cause that you may be bound up, you have no healing medicines. ... For I have wounded

you with the wound of an enemy, with the chastisement of a cruel one, for the multitude of your iniquities, because your sins have increased. ... Your sorrow is incurable. ... I will restore you to health." (Jeremiah 30:12-14, 17)

FOOTNOTES:

Again, you will find it helpful to read these and jot down what they mean to you.

[1] Jeremiah 30:1- 12

[2] Jeremiah 30: 17

[3] Jeremiah 30: 24

JOURNALING QUESTIONS:

1. Are you in a personal wilderness now? If so, describe it.

_____

_____

_____

_____

_____

2. What do you think led you into it?

_____

_____

_____

_____

3. What will it take to get you out?

_____

_____

_____

_____

_____

4. What responsibility must you assume for this wilderness?

_____

_____

_____

_____

_____

CHAPTER 5

HEALING WATERS

HEALING. IT IS ALMOST A trite word today because so many of us know we need healing. Unscrupulous people use the word to describe their counseling methods, behavior modification techniques, and just about anything else they want to promote.

Other people claim healing is a cop-out, a flight from personal responsibility. Some so-called Bible believing Christians, ignoring the simple plain truth of scriptures, use convoluted Bible interpretations to maintain that God no longer heals today. Our world, like perhaps no other, has been doing its own thing for a long time now. That is why it cries out so desperately for healing.

Healing was central to the message and work of Jesus of Nazareth, and not just physical healing. Healing virtue flowed from Him, like rivers of living water. And the healing he offers us goes beyond the physical. In fact, He said it was the very reason He came to earth. Not just to give us a free ticket to Heaven, but to heal the broken hearted, release those who were bruised by life, and to set the captives free.

The very name Christ is intimately related to this mission of healing the broken. As I said in the last chapter, He came to fulfill the prophecy Jeremiah had made centuries before. The Lord Himself would heal our pain.

We live in an age where we realize that the greatest pain is emotional. Healing our pain has become a national obsession, as well it should remain. For, many of us, unless we receive the healing for which we hunger, we will be emotionally crippled.

Hampered from becoming all we can be, and perhaps even eventually unable to function productively in society.

Even many Christians find themselves becoming deeply bitter and cynical. It's one thing to know that rivers of living water should flow from us, that we are to be instruments of God's healing and redemptive love, and quite another to tap into fast underground spring of the river of life.

It is then that the wilderness does its work. In the Old Testament, the Jews wandered across a howling wilderness for forty years in their quest for the Promised Land. It was forty years of arid struggle, painful frustration, and humiliating failure.

Forty years of subsistence living and forty years of knowing that there was something far better, a land of abundance and prosperity, a land that they were unable to even see, let alone inherit. Perhaps there is a reason why forty years seems to be a particularly painful reality check for most of us.

The wilderness wanderings of the ancient Jews symbolize an experience we must all go through as we seek the most from life. Our personal wilderness, like the vast, daunting wilderness faced by the ancient Israelites, is designed to test and humble us, to show us our own heart, to see if we'll obey God, or insist on doing things in our own stubborn way.

Yet the purpose for the wilderness isn't just to humble and test us. God intends to use it for our good [1]. For indeed, the only way to enter His promised land of peace, abundance, love, joy, and prosperity is through the howling wilderness.

It purges, tempers, refines, and strengthens us like fine steel or precious metal, enabling us to conquer the inner enemies that would seek to rob us of our Kingdom inheritance. This is the baptism of fire Jesus spoke of.

Wilderness trials bring to the surface the things that need to be healed, in order for us to become obedient, so we can then be blessed with an abundant life.

In Jeremiah 30, the Lord promises to save His people from their captivity. He says He will free them from the grip of their enemies, and restore them to the land of promise that they lost because of their rebellion.

This passage is not just referring to the ancient Jews. As we have seen, it is also relevant at the end of time. He also tells us that for this to be accomplished He must first heal our pain.

Only then can we obey Him. Only then can we truly receive His promises of abundant love, abiding peace, and everlasting joy. Only then can our lives be rebuilt on His sure foundation so we can again receive His blessing [2].

This section of the workbook will introduce you to the healing possibilities that the Lord promised us in the last days. After you have prayerfully answered each question to the best of your ability, invite the Lord to touch what He wants to heal in you today.

As you do this, you will find Him faithfully working to get at the roots of the pain that has bound you. You will also discover that He loves you more than you ever knew.

SCRIPTURE TO MEDITATE ON THIS WEEK:

"And you shall remember that the Lord your God led you all the way these 40 years in the wilderness, to humble you and test you, to know what was in your heart, whether you would keep His commandments. ... (He) fed you in the wilderness with manna, ... that He might humble you and that He might test you, to do good for you in the end... and you shall remember the Lord your God, for it is He who gives you power to get wealth, that He may establish His covenant which He swore to your fathers, as it is this day." (Deuteronomy 8: 2, 16, 18)

FOOTNOTES:

[1] Deuteronomy 8

[2] Jeremiah 30:17-22

JOURNALING QUESTIONS:

1. What wilderness experiences are you encountering in your life right now?

_____

_____

_____

_____

_____

2. Where do you feel defeated? What besetting sins have you been unable to overcome?

_____

_____

_____

_____

_____

3. What are the most painful things you can remember in your life?

_____

_____

_____

_____

_____

4. On separate paper, take time to journal on each of these events, letting your pen flow freely as you do. Resist the temptation to edit your thoughts and feelings, just pour them all out as openly as you can. God already knows how you feel. Unless you choose to share it with someone, no one needs to read this but you.

   For each painful incident, express what happened to you in as much detail as you can. If strong feelings come up as you do this do not suppress them, let them come fully to the surface. If you need to cry, shout, or in other ways ventilate these feelings do so.

Tell God exactly how you feel about these things and even about Him. His shoulders are broad, He will understand and He will not judge you for your feelings.

Now look again at your besetting sins.

Read I John 1:9. **Notice that the only precondition for receiving forgiveness is confession. You need not promise that from now on your obedience will be perfect. You need not even repent. I know myself too well to make glib promises of repentance, for repentance itself is not something you can manufacture, it is something that God alone can grant (cf. II Timothy 2:25).**

Then pray this prayer: *"Dear Father in Heaven, forgive me for everything I've done to offend You in these situations. And forgive me for the many times I have tried and failed to overcome my sins. I can't promise that I'll never do them again, only that in my heart of hearts, I don't want to keep sinning. I am grateful that You look on my heart and not my outer appearance. Wash the broken parts of me with Your healing waters. Deepen the good work that You've begun in me and give me Your patience for this healing journey. You said You would continue this work until I die or Jesus returns (cf. Philippians 1:6). Let Your gentleness make me great (Psalm 18:35), and give me the faith to receive whatever healing You have for me today. Thank you, Lord. In Jesus' precious name. Amen."*

(If you have a hard time praying in Jesus' name, you do not have to. But you may want to read the chapter entitled "Why Jesus Should Be Your Higher Power" now to understand why I recommend it.)

CHAPTER 6

THE PROBLEM IS YOUR WON'T POWER

WHY IS IT SO HARD TO OBEY? How come it is so difficult to break destructive habits? Why does it sometimes seem that the harder we try to do right the more difficult it is?

I knew a man who owned an old hump-backed 1950 vintage Mercury. On the back of it was written, "The hurrier I go the behinder I get." That has often described my greatest attempts at being the best person I can be.

The answers to these questions can be found in the very nature of what it means to be a true Christian. All the laws in the Bible can be summed up in one word; Love [1]. We are called to love God above everything and love our neighbor as ourselves. If we can learn to love, we will fulfill every mandate God has for us, simple right?

Simple, yet very, very difficult. I wish all I had to do to be faithful was keep a few club house rules, break all my bad habits, keep my nose clean, stop swearing, and just be a general nice guy, but it's not that easy.

God commands us to love, and love can be the toughest thing in the world to do.

When I first became a Christian, I thought love would be a snap. After all, I was a romantic. I knew how to buy a girl flowers and take her out for a nice dinner.

Yet, I soon learned that the love God is talking about is not being in love, it simply loves. It is not romance, its reality, not because of, but in spite of, and that is quite a different matter.

Love is always selfless, always concerned not for its own needs but for the highest good of the beloved. Love is patient, kind, unselfish, never greedy, or self-seeking. Love endures rejection, it is not demanding, and is never ornery or impatient [2].

I was soon to learn that I was not very good at love. The first Christian girl to spurn my affections made me very hard to live with. Her rejection plunged me into almost suicidal despair. Why did this happen to me? Years later I would learn a profound truth that would forever change my life.

It is as hard for a person with a broken heart to love, as it is for a person with a broken foot to run.

My heart had been broken a few times since early adolescence. If I were going to be able to love, I had to first be healed of at least some of the hurts I had experienced over the years.

As a young Christian, I was surprised to learn that Jesus did not just live and die to get me to Heaven. As I have mentioned earlier, the very reason Christ was anointed was to heal the broken hearted, bind up the bruised, and set the captives free. This was central to His destiny. That is because unless we allow Him to do that for us we can never hope to truly obey Him. It would be impossible for us to love.

The Jews didn't recognize Him as their Messiah because they expected the Messiah to save them from the Romans, as an earthly king would. Many Christians struggle with their faith because they think Jesus is only a heavenly king. That He merely came to get them to heaven.

The good news of Christ's kingdom is it's both, and it pertains to this life as well as the next. In reality, His kingdom is not of this world, yet paradoxically, it is also an inner personal kingdom [3]. That's how He becomes the savior who will save us from our sins [4].

He does this by healing the inner brokenness that makes us vulnerable to sin. He does this as we allow Him to rule, not just Rome or Jerusalem, but also to establish His kingship within us, in our heart of hearts.

The heart is many things, one of which is it's the seat of our desires. Jesus said that all the things that corrupt our life and interfere with our well-being flow out of the heart [5]. **In a real sense, the heart of our problem is the problem of our heart. When our heart is broken, our desires are warped, and that is dangerous.**

As someone wisely said, we develop longings that can shorten our lives. We yearn for things that not only can't truly satisfy us, but may in fact destroy us. A broken heart can fuel lust, rage, hatred, envy, strife, all the attitudinal sins that defile our life and relationships.

When I led my first healing workshop in a prison, I asked the men how many saw a relationship between mishandled emotions and the crimes that landed them in prison. Every hand went up.

Unless something intervenes to help us break the pattern of disobedience, we cultivate self-destructive appetites. Like Orwell's predictions in 1984, the things we do to set us free enslave us. We become shackled to our sins. We no longer have bad habits, they have us, and if this persists, there is seemingly very little we can do about it.

That is why Jesus said that anyone who willfully disobeys the Lord becomes enslaved to sin [6]. This is our spiritual captivity, and it is every bit as difficult to break free from as the bondage the Jews were in.

It's not our will power that's the problem, it's our won't power. We become hopelessly addicted to the bad we don't wish to do, and we somehow can't bring ourselves to do the good that we should. This is part and parcel of our human condition. I take comfort in knowing that even the Apostle Paul struggled with this [7].

To make matters worse, our suffering increases as we indulge in our sinful attitudes. There is a direct correlation between our sin and our suffering [8]. The more we suffer the more we seek comfort from our favorite sin. Be it through abusing drugs, sex, alcohol, food, rage, work, self-righteousness, or religion, we crave the most available, most effective emotional opiate for our own self-medication.

Some compulsions may seem more harmless than others but they aren't. I was shocked to learn that the children of a work addict manifest the same symptoms as the children of an alcoholic. The work addict's mommy or daddy is just as absent from the child as the alcoholic's.

The only difference being the addiction is to work instead of the bottle, and how do you fault that? You don't commend an alcoholic for being a wonderful drunk, but work addiction is different. It is what I call the acceptable addiction. It is the one compulsion most of us loudly applaud.

Whatever a person's favorite escape from reality, it dulls our pain and offer us temporary respite from our suffering, but the problem doesn't end there. It is not only our sins of commission that bind us; our problem is also compounded by our sins of omission.

What I mean is this. Righteousness is the only thing that truly fulfills us. When I became a Christian, I realized for the first time in my life that it truly is more blessed to give than receive. That is what righteousness is all about.

It is much more than the absence of wrong. Righteousness is the love of God made tangible in response to human need. It is the positive expression of God's love flowing through us to help one another. It's what we are made for, the only thing that truly satisfies our deepest longings.

When we are bound by sin, we not only do what we should not, but we also do not do what we should. What will fill our emptiness. We will not risk love because it's too dangerous and it may cause us more pain.

Locked in a prison of selfishness, we are unable to be free from the things that are harming us or do the things that would help us. That is why we need healing for the pain that binds us. It is the very thing that Jesus came to earth to give us.

That is why He was anointed by healing our brokenness; he liberates us from the effects of our wounds, and sets us free from our captivity to sin. This explains why those very things comprised His life's mission statement.

Without His healing, we simply cannot love we can only lust. Without loving, we not only can't obey Him, but we also can't receive the abundant life He came to give us (9) (Cf. John 10:10).

My life mission is to learn how to love and teach others to love. When I became involved with healing, I thought it was a distraction from this purpose. I soon learned that it is not. It may in fact be the only way I can fulfill it.

Far from being a flight from responsibility, spiritual healing is the only thing that can release us to be truly responsible. It is the only way to free us to do God's will.

In reality, not just in theory, this is the one thing that can set us free. As we become more healed, we find it easier to obey the Lord. We can better live by the benevolent laws of His Kingdom. We can give ourselves unreservedly to learning how to love. We can, in fact, make earth like Heaven. This is precisely why He gave powerful healing gifts to His Church.

SCRIPTURE TO MEDITATE ON THIS WEEK:

"Love is patient, love is kind, and is not jealous; love does not brag and is not arrogant, does not act unbecomingly; it does not seek its own, is not provoked, does not take into account a wrong suffered, does not rejoice in unrighteousness, but rejoices with the truth; bears all things, believes all things, hopes all things, endures all things. Love never fails." (I Corinthians 13: 4-8a, NASB)

Here is an interesting exercise. Substitute your name every place in the above passage that uses the word love. Ken is patient... kind... etc. How did you measure up?

FOOTNOTES:

[1] I Timothy 1:5

[2] I Corinthians 13 - the entire chapter

[3] Luke 17:21

[4] Matthew 1:21

[5] Mark 7:1-23

[6] John 8:31-36

[7] Romans 7:14-25

[8] I Peter 4:1-2

[9] John 10:10

JOURNALING QUESTIONS:

1. Where has your will power failed you?

_____

_____

_____

_____

_____

2. What does the phrase "The law of sin and death" mean to you?

_____

_____

_____

_____

_____

3. If you could ask the Lord to free you from any compulsion, to totally deliver you from any destructive behavior, what would it be?

_____

_____

_____

_____

_____

CHAPTER 7

RESTORING THE SOUL

O FTEN, TREATMENT, EVEN HOLISTIC healing, is only partially effective because it's based on an incomplete under-standing of the nature of man. If we're to do better than this, we must treat the whole person.

Only then can we make people truly healthy, only then can we help them to become more whole. Any part of the personality we ignore will leave the job only partially complete and set the stage for greater problems.

The deep, inner nature of a person is the prime case in point. Man isn't just his body, but neither is he only body and soul combined. As God is revealed in three distinct forms, Father, Son, and Holy Spirit, so is man. According to the Bible, man is comprised of three parts, body, soul, and spirit [1].

Obviously, the body is the physical part of man. However, the metaphysical portion, that part which transcends the physical, is made up of two distinct parts, spirit and soul. Each is very different and requires special understanding.

Concerning our spiritual nature, the Bible teaches two important things. First, God is a Spirit [2], and second, man is made in His image [3]. That means we're created to be like God. We are spiritual beings. The neglect or misunderstanding of the spiritual nature of man is responsible for much human suffering.

The human spirit is that part of each of us which is capable of being united with God. Yet, because we have all gone our own way and done our own thing, our spirits are deadened by what the Bible calls sin.

Sin is perhaps the most misunderstood term in religion. Linguistically, it does not always refer to some terrible misbehavior. The literal meaning of sin is falling short of God's glory.

This metaphor is one of aiming at a target and not reaching it. The target we're to aim at is the glory of God. This brings us to another misunderstood term. Just what is the glory of God?

God doesn't have an ego problem. This is not saying we should refrain from evil, or do well, so that He looks good. God IS good, He does not need us to make Him look good.

The glory of God in the Old Testament was called Shekinah. When people experienced it they literally glowed. Another way to describe this divine shine is radiant living, or living gloriously.

This is a magnificent experiencing of life in all its fullness. We've perhaps all glimpsed people who live like that, full of fire, love, and enthusiasm. Sound good? You bet it is.

When we intentionally follow the ways of sin, or inglorious living, we live beneath ourselves as spiritual beings made in God's image. I liken it to buying into a counterfeit view of reality, one that is both inadequate and inaccurate.

When we invite the Lord to come in and take control of our lives, His Spirit, the Holy Spirit, gives new life to our spirit. In this way, His fullness fills our emptiness and we become new people.

We are so transformed by this experience that the only way to adequately describe it is to liken it to being born again. We change so much we become totally new people.

A metaphor that's often used for the Holy Spirit is oil. In a very real way, like lamp oil, His spiritual energy source lights up our lives. That's why we glow.

This is the beginning of truly becoming like God. Before this experience we all bear His image, but without His Spirit we don't have the necessary substance to enable us to fulfill the potential of that image.

We're like a car without gas, a house without electricity, a being without the power to become truly alive to all of life's possibilities and realities. The indwelling Presence of God's Spirit gives us the capacity to live like Him as well. It provides the key energy that's essential for glorious, radiant living.

This is the key to the ultimate fulfillment of our human potential. When, at our invitation, His Spirit unites with ours, He enables us to truly be all we can be and do all we can do. It's the beginning of a whole new life. One lived as a prince or princess of the King of Kings and an heir to His spectacular Kingdom.

The third part of man, the soul, is different from our spirit. The soul has wisely been called the chairman of the board of our personality. It mediates the relationship between the Spirit of God within us and the urges and desires of our physical body. It's like the referee who decides which one wins in the event of a conflict of wills.

However the soul is more than that. It's also the very essence of who we are. It's what gives us our unique identity and personality, making us different from every other person on the earth.

As God and man are both tripartite, so also is the soul comprised of three unique parts. These are the intellect, emotions, and will. The soul contains the part of us that has been wounded by life, bruised by hurts, and damaged by sin. It's the part of us that must be restored [4] if we are to become healthy, whole people.

The problem with both religion and talk therapy is that each only works on a part of the soul, leaving the job of total restoration only partly done.

As we've seen, good religion begins by changing our spirit and giving it new life. That's wonderful, even essential. It's probably the ultimate peak experience in all of life. Yet it's not enough to make us completely whole.

The soul needs restoration as well, and both secular therapy and religious counseling usually only affect the intellect and the will.

Churches, self-help books, and therapists offer people piles of words to impact their minds. They also try to alter people's will, bring them to repentance, and change their values and direction in life. These things are good as far as they go. But that's the problem. They don't go far enough. They leave the job of self-transformation unfinished.

Both religion and traditional therapy only impact two-thirds of the soul, the intellect and will. Two-thirds is just sixty-six percent, barely a passing grade. Neither religion, nor therapy rarely impact the emotional damage we've received, and this is where our greatest hurts reside.

As we've seen, the Lord promised to heal all our diseases. That includes the dis-eases of the soul, the things that have harmed our emotional life. This is the area that Jeremiah addressed when he promised that the Lord would cure our incurable wound, that He would heal our pain [5].

It's what Jesus referred to when He said that our Heavenly Father had anointed Him to bind up the broken-hearted and set at liberty the bruised [6]. This was essential to His earthly mission. These few simple promises contain some of the best news He has to offer in this life.

Even secular science today acknowledges the amazing interrelationship between the physical body and our emotions. In our work, we have seen this as well. By ministering to people's emotional hurts we've seen people healed of migraine headaches, seizures, colitis, cancerous lumps, chronic fatigue, Crones disease, and many other physiological afflictions. We've also been successful in treating more traditional emotionally based problems like eating disorders, sexual addictions and orientations, alcoholism, and work addiction.

We've even seen the Lord heal severe problems like multiple personality disorder, post-traumatic stress disorder, and numerous varieties of neuroses and psychoses. The things we have learned are remarkably simple yet profoundly powerful. It boils down to this:

When we heal the root pain that underlies these disorders, the symptoms and the compulsive behaviors people use to get relief usually just disappear.

Probably the most dramatic example of this came when we were beginning to conduct our "Liberating the Wounded" seminars. These seminars were designed to equip churches to heal the hurting in their congregations by using the spiritual gifts of their own people.

We had been invited to a rural church where many wonderful and powerful things happened, but the one I shall always remember involved a sweet middle-aged woman. She obviously had some severe medical conditions that made it hard for her to walk, talk, and function normally.

They had taken such a toll on her body that I thought she was near sixty years old when I met her. I was shocked to learn that she was only forty-six.

After one of the afternoon sessions she came up to me and said, "Pastor, I really enjoyed the ministry I received today and I feel much better, but I obviously need a lot of physical healing. Can this kind of ministry help me with that as well?

I was on the spot. Looking at her gnarled body I was overwhelmed by her needs. I was also, uncharacteristically, at a complete loss for words. I did the only thing I knew to do. I asked her a question, biding for time, praying for wisdom.

Do you believe the Lord can heal you? I asked. "Of course," she replied. "He can heal anything, she said. But why would He want to heal me?"

I had my way out. The only thing I knew to tell her was, "I want to suggest that you ask the Lord to prove to you that He loves you and would want to heal you."

"Okay," she said. "Thank you very much," and she left. I was off the hook.

That evening, after another full night of ministry, the pastor, his wife, our team, and the lady went out for pizza. We placed our order, but before it came the woman began having seizures. I quickly prayed for her and sent someone to call an ambulance.

She was turning gray and other sickly colors I'd never seen in a person. I had no faith that our prayers were doing her any good. After what seemed like an interminable time the EMS unit finally showed up.

They quickly hooked her up to life support and rushed her to a nearby hospital, barely breathing. We were all really shook up, none more than me. I felt like Satan had counterattacked us, and our efforts to fight him were useless.

'Maybe we traumatized her during the ministry time,' I mused to myself. 'Maybe we made her problems worse. Maybe she'll die!' It sure looked like she could.

Then I got mad at God. On the way back to the hotel we had quite a conversation. Actually, it was a monologue. 'You got me into this,' I told Him. 'I don't want to do this any more. I just want to go home and become a pastor again.'

I had a hard time sleeping that night, and an even tougher time getting up to preach the next morning. Even though there were more glorious testimonies of the healings and deliverances people had received the previous day, all I could think about was the lady in the hospital. Somehow, I finished my sermon and went home.

Two weeks later the pastor came to see me. Before I even hung up his jacket I asked, "How's that woman who went to the hospital?"

His answer astonished me. "She's wonderful! I've probably seen her go through fifty healing lines in all the years I've known her and nothing ever helped her like your seminar."

"Wait a minute," I said. "We can't be talking about the same person. The lady I'm referring to was in ICU when I left."

"Oh that," he said, like it was no big deal. "What happened was that she had received so much healing at the afternoon session that when she went to take her normal dose of medication it was too much for her and she overdosed. They cut back on her medicine by two-thirds and she's fine now, radiant with the love of God and a real testimony to the Lord and your ministry."

I'd always known that there was an enormous link between the emotional and physical. Any honest doctor will tell you that probably 90% of his patients have no clear pathological reason for their illnesses, but here was living proof of the connection. What's better, here was proof that He could indeed heal all our diseases, body, soul and spirit.

I've seen the woman since then, and what her pastor said was true. Though she wasn't yet completely healed, and she had a long way to go, she was visibly better, and her spirit and attitude toward life were remarkable.

In the healing the Lord did for her, He had persuaded her of His profound love for her. That revelation alone guaranteed that she would never be the same.

There is nothing God can't heal, but if we want to become whole, we must treat the whole person, body, soul, and spirit, as well as bring healing to the entire soul, intellect, emotions and will. Once we learn to do that we can talk about total healing. Better yet we can experience it and share it with others. For

God uses wounded healers to heal others and it's even more rewarding to share it with others than it is to receive it for ourselves.

SCRIPTURE TO MEDITATE ON THIS WEEK:

"The Lord is my shepherd, I shall not want ... He restores my soul." (Psalm 23:1, 3a)

In what way do you want Him to restore your soul?

FOOTNOTES:

[4] I Thessalonians 5:23

[5] I John 4:24

[6] Genesis 1:27

[7] Psalm 23:3

[8] Jeremiah 30

[9] Luke 4:16-18

JOURNALING QUESTIONS:

1. Are there any physical symptoms for which you'd like healing? If so, what?

_____

_____

_____

_____

_____

2. When did these symptoms begin?

_____

_____

_____

_____

_____

3. What was going on in your life at the time they began?

_____

_____

_____

_____

_____

4. Write out exactly what you would like to ask the Lord to do for you and commit it to Him in prayer.

_____

_____

_____

_____

_____

5. What things, if any, make it hard for you to believe He will heal you?

_____

_____

_____

_____

_____

6. Read Mark 11:22-26 and Mark 9:23-24. If you need help with your unbelief ask the Lord for help until you get it. If you don't give up, He will either help you directly or make you aware of what you will need to do to receive His help. He wants you healed.

CHAPTER 8

WHO DID THIS TO YOU?

S O, LET'S REVIEW WHAT WE'VE learned. Unresolved pain keeps us in bondage to sin and self, preventing us from having a radiant life. The sins we commit wound us further [1], and our wounds often prompt us to sin more. So, sin reinforces its power over us, creating a downward spiral of pain, addiction, and bondage until [2] we are imprisoned by our own insatiable lusts.

Both the sins of commission and sins of omission can harm us. The sins of commission, things like abusing food, sex, drugs, work, etc., anesthetize our pain. Sins of omission, like refusing to care, risk, or forgive, also keep us enslaved.

Both types of sin guarantee that we can no longer do what we want or be who we truly are. We're too busy feeding our addictions, or avoiding pains, to live, enjoy life, and become all we can be.

This sets up another major problem, a key roadblock in the pursuit of happiness. We become afraid to love, and love is the very thing we were created for. Here's what I mean.

God is the very essence of Love. Since we're made in His image, we're made to be like Him. We can only fulfill our destiny by learning how to love. Until we truly learn how to love, until we come outside of our own little world enough to let God love the hurting and broken world through us, we will never truly know fulfillment.

Let me repeat, love is what we were made for. Nothing else truly satisfies the longings of our broken hearts. Until we are free to love we are still in chains, bound by fear and anxiety.

This, in turn, presents us with yet another problem. No one escapes life unscathed. We've all been hurt when we've attempted to love.

More likely, we've been hurt not so much by loving, but rather by trying to get our own needs for love met or by trying to avoid being hurt.

Often this pain is worsened when it comes from the hands of family, friends, loved ones, or others who believe as we do. Any rejection is terrible, but it especially hurts when it's done by people from whom we expected to receive the pure love of God. Unfortunately this has happened to us all. We are all, what I call, burned-again Christians (or Jews, or Muslims, and so on).

I began to sense that rejection was a big issue for me. As I got in touch with my feelings, in certain circumstances I realized I was really reacting to any situation where rejection was a possibility.

I didn't know how huge the problem was until I completed a simple exercise. I decided to write down all the times I could remember having experienced rejection. When I was done it filled two whole pages!

On those pages were the times I'd felt hurt when my affections were spurned by prospective girlfriends. There was the thirteen year-old who broke my heart when I was thirteen; the fourteen year old who left me in shock, trading me for a pimple faced loser, when I was sixteen. That one hurt in places I didn't know I had.

I hurt so bad I could hardly eat or sleep. Then there was the love of my life, the young woman I asked to marry me after I became a Christian. When she turned me down, it was all I could do to keep from driving my car into a telephone pole.

Yet not all of my hurts and rejections were romantic, not all of them were even things people chose to do to me. The worst hurt in my entire life was prompted by the sudden, unexpected death of my grandfather when I was ten.

It took me twenty-two years to finish grieving his death.

There was also the time I lost an election in college; the time I got black-balled from a fraternity because I took a girl to homecoming that one of the brothers wanted to ask; the time a major corporation turned me down for a job.

In spite of it all though, the most damaging hurts came at the hands of my Christian brothers and sisters. There were the people in the first ministry I worked for who passed me over for a leadership role in lieu of another, less talented, guy. They did this because his personality was less abrasive than mine. There were the Charismatic Christians who left the first church I pastored because, though I too was charismatic, I insisted that they exercise their spiritual gifts in an orderly manner. All over town, they said I had squelched the Holy Spirit.

Then there was the guy I'd led to the Lord who then tried to run me out of my own church. He believed the distortions of a woman, who I had stood up to, when she tried to manipulate the board of our church.

I also had a close friend who tried to undermine my ministry, and a couple whose marriage and business I had helped save who spread lies about me all over town. I could go on but I won't. You get the picture. Like someone once said, some of God's sheep have funny teeth!

Why am I telling you these things? It is not because I want, or need, your pity. Pity parties are no fun, no one else wants to attend! I'm telling you this because we all have lots of times in our lives when we've been let down, rejected, and desperately hurt by mates, parents, siblings, children, trusted friends, colleagues, and associates.

Those situations hurt like hell itself. Untreated, they can leave us wounded, bruised, and permanently scarred, afraid to ever risk loving again.

This is the real reason why every Bible school and seminary I know counsels prospective pastors to refrain from friendships within their churches. They offer lofty reasons for this, but the bottom line is it's safer to remain aloof. Your survival is more assured. Secular therapists are given the same sorry advice, don't get close to a client, you'll lose your objectivity.

However, the things people need if they're going to get healthy are sincere love, authentic warmth, and genuine affection. As Dr. Karl Menninger said, love is the true medicine the world needs to cure its manifold ills.

But there's something even more important to our health and well-being than receiving love. The one thing we need to learn more than anything else if we're to become happy and whole is how to give love. Unless we love, we can never be free or happy. He who loves is born of God [3].

True Christian love requires giving. I used to think that the King James translation, which uses charity as the word for love, was outdated. It isn't. You can give without loving but you can't love without giving.

As my favorite poet says, "you give but little when you give of your possessions, it's when you give of yourself that you truly give"{Kahlil Gibran, The Prophet]. This is exactly what the Lord recommended when He said we must give of ourselves to the poor and needy [4].

The poor need more than a hand out; they need someone to give of themselves. Only love can compensate for the years of neglect, abuse, and emotional deprivation that have starved their very souls.

Those who must live with excruciating emotional pain can't love. A man with a severe toothache can think of no one but himself. This is even truer of a person with a tortured soul. That's why it was so important for Jesus to heal our pain. It's why He promised to bind up the broken-hearted and to set at liberty the bruised.

Unless we let Him do that for us, we can't love. Unless we love, we won't have an abundant life, no matter how much gusto we try to grab on the way through.

We are made to love. Nothing else can satisfy our deepest yearnings, nothing less fulfills us. Without love, we just "can't get no (from Rollin Stones song) satisfaction."

So here's what we're dealing with. Hurts from our past make us hyper-sensitive to rejection, afraid to love, and reluctant to risk as we must in order to do the Lord's will.

After all, Jesus got killed for loving people who were hurting, and we instinctively know that love will also require our selfishness to die. That's too risky if you're living in a world of hurt.

So how do we heal the pain from our past? Now we are ready to answer that question, but we must start with some important issues. We must identify the hurt places in each of us that need to be healed.

SCRIPTURES TO MEDITATE ON THIS WEEK:

"He who loves is born of God." (I John 4:7)

"Is this not the fast that I have chosen: To loose the bonds of wickedness, To undo the heavy burdens, To let the oppressed go free, And that you break every yoke? Is it not to share your bread with the hungry, And that you bring to your house the poor who are cast out; When you see the naked, that you cover him, And not to hide yourself from your own flesh? Then your light shall spring forth like the morning, And your healing shall spring forth speedily." (Isaiah 58:6-8a)

FOOTNOTES:

[1] Jeremiah 30:14, Psalm 139:23-24

[2] Romans 7:7-20, John 8:31-36

[3] I John 4:7

[4] Isaiah 58:6-10

JOURNALING QUESTIONS:

1. List the times you were rejected romantically. Include every one you remember from the most recent to the earliest.

_____

_____

_____

_____

_____

2. How are those hurts affecting your love life now?

_____

_____

_____

_____

_____

3. What other losses, hurts and rejections can you remember in each of these areas?

   a. Family: Include parents, grandparents, siblings, cousins, aunts and uncles, and anyone else who lived with you as a child.

_____

_____

_____

_____

b. Friends: Include preschool, elementary and secondary school, college, neighbor children, and adult friends who may have hurt and betrayed you.

_____

_____

_____

_____

_____

c. How have those in authority hurt you? Include teachers, pastors, coaches, activity sponsors, parents of friends and neighbor's, police, bosses, and anyone else you can think of. (Now do you see why you have a problem with authority?)

_____

_____

_____

_____

_____

d. Now include the names of any in the religious community who hurt you at various times in your life. Remember pastors, youth leaders, choir directors, Sunday school teachers, etc.

_____

_____

_____

_____

_____

4. How has this affected your ability to trust God?

_____

_____

_____

_____

_____

5. What is the most painful memory you have of rejection? Write out what happened and how you feel about the person or people involved. If strong feelings surface take time for them, experience them, and let them run their course.

Then write each of these people from category 4 a letter, one you will never send, telling them what they did and explaining exactly how you feel. Don't edit it. No one needs to read this but you.

Use whatever language you need to fully express your feelings and make the letter as long as you need it to be. Just let your pen flow freely until you are emptied out. Do this on separate paper, you may need a lot.

Also on separate paper, write another letter to the Lord. Tell Him how you feel about these things, and how you feel about Him. Whether you feel He let you down, or didn't protect you, or anything else you feel.

When you are done, ask Him to begin healing the hurt, changing your heart, and removing any lingering resentment or bitterness. Pray, as King David suggests, for His gentleness to make you great.

Finally, ask Him to give you the wisdom, grace, compassion, and insight to forgive, from your heart, those people who have wronged or harmed you. Remember to include the Lord in this. He hasn't sinned, but you may be holding something against Him. If you find it impossible to forgive someone, don't worry about this now, just make note of it. We will deal with that later.

CHAPTER 9

HOW DO YOU HEAL DAMAGED EMOTIONS?

Now that we know what's been damaged and what caused the damage, we're ready to explore how to heal it. Even though the revelations that surfaced in the last exercises are useful, they don't yet heal the pain.

Scientists have proven that every memory we have ever had is indelibly recorded somewhere in the brain. A certain portion of the brain stores not only each memory we've had but also all the feelings associated with it.

A simple experiment proved this. When the brain is opened and an electrode touched to a part of it, every time that same spot is touched the person will recall the event that is stored there and re-experience all the feelings associated with it.

I know everything we've done is recorded in the brain. When I was seventeen years old I had a root canal on two of my front teeth. I had been hit in the mouth playing football, and again in the same place playing water polo.

The roots had to be removed. When the roots were pulled from my head, I passed out. While I was unconscious, I thought

I was out for 90 minutes. My whole life passed before my eyes, every event I had experienced since birth. I was shocked to learn that I had been out for only about 90 seconds.

Every event we've experienced is recorded in that marvelous, fleshy video tape player we call the brain. Someday, on that great, eternal instant replay, it will be replayed for the entire world to see [1]. Whether we remember them or not, those stored experiences affect our life, even the events we've forgotten.

Just because you've forgotten that you stored some vegetables in the pantry won't keep them from smelling up the kitchen when they rot, and just because we can't recall what happened to us doesn't mean it's lost the power to pollute our life.

Again, time doesn't heal any wounds; it just makes them recede back into our subconscious. As someone once said, if time heals, God is unnecessary.

We only consciously recall about ten percent of the things that happen to us. This is the proverbial tip of the iceberg. The other ninety percent is buried beneath the surface of our life, in that great reservoir of hurts and broken dreams called the subconscious.

Is this accurate? Is this revelation biblically solid or just more psychobabble? The distinction is of utmost importance to me. I've had my fill of false, untested theories and you probably have also.

To answer that question let me tell you about my mid-life crisis. I didn't believe in mid-life crises, but when I had one around the age of forty I decided to go to a monastery in Nebraska for a two-week intensive healing retreat. I learned some amazing things there.

For years I felt there was something important about the biblical concept of the heart that I had not understood something essential to healing. There I learned what it was. What the Bible calls the heart is what psychologists refer to as the unconscious.

This is incredibly important. Jesus said all the things that defile us come from the heart [2]. The apostle Paul alluded to this when he said sin is lodged within us [3], sin that prompts us to do what we hate and keeps us from doing good [4].

Many of the things that harm us from the inside are long since forgotten. That's why talk therapy is so limited in its ability to help us. We only consciously remember ten percent of the things that have happened to us. Therefore, it can only treat ten percent of the things we need to heal and resolve.

Ninety percent of the things that happened to us are buried in our heart, or the unconscious.

What do we do with that other ninety percent? You can see why people are so excited about our retreats and seminars. We use and teach techniques that surface the hidden things of the heart, the ninety percent that are forgotten. We then give people tools and experiences to heal them.

This is incredibly valuable. A dear friend of mine who is a top professional athlete attended our basic retreat some years ago. She said it did more for her than twenty years of sports psychology.

So how does the Lord heal the hidden hurts of the heart? The best metaphor I know of for healing emotional pain is related to frostbite.

When I was a boy, my suburb flooded vacant lots in the winter so we could ice skate. Like most young boys, I was impervious to pain when I was having fun. I'd stay out in the cold playing hockey until I could no longer feel my hands and feet.

Minor frostbite set in. When I got home I learned that though I felt very cold, the best way to treat the frostbite wasn't to plunge my hands and feet into hot water, but to start by running cool water over them. Then gradually turn up the temperature to lukewarm and eventually to hot.

As I did this, the feeling would gradually return to my extremities. When they did, I would go from feeling total numbness, then pain, and then normal again. My feeling and sensitivity returned only after I endured the pain.

The same thing happens with emotional pain. If it isn't properly resolved we become numb to it. A part of us is sealed off from our feelings. This explains why so many people are insensitive to others.

Just this morning a friend shared with me how he had felt totally shut off from his feelings as a boy. He was raised in a strict religious home that invalidated his feelings. He said he learned to shut out all negative feelings and act as if they didn't exist.

After a retreat, he came home and began to feel and express his anger, hurt, and shame. It was the beginning of a profound healing, for just as a doctor can only treat a visible wound, we can only heal what we can feel.

Remember when I said there's no such thing as a sin that doesn't hurt anyone? We live in an age where sin abounds, and where sin abounds pain abounds. The legacy of all that unhealed pain is an increasingly insensitive society, one where people frequently hurt each other without even caring or even realizing it.

However, God didn't plan it this way. He created our emotions to function remarkably well. They are meant to work for us, to help us, to prevent us from even needing much healing.

A young child can fall and hurt himself and scream so loud you fear that he or she must certainly need something amputated, but within a couple of minutes the child is playing again as if nothing had ever happened. Why?

Tiny children haven't learned to bury their feelings, they haven't discovered that it isn't safe to feel and express their hurts. They cry out their pain and in so doing not only cleanse the emotional hurt but start the natural healing process.

Tears actually remove toxic chemicals from the body.

Think about what's happened to us when we've spent years suppressing those tears. They don't just go away, they stay within us, fueling our compulsions and often even our physical diseases. Many today recognize that pain is somehow stored in the body at a cellular level.

Most of us stopped crying a long time ago. Or we cry but never get release from the pain because we have never learned how to truly bring it to the surface where it can be resolved.

It doesn't take long as children to discover we will be ridiculed if we cry while on the playground. We're taught that big boys don't cry. Adults may even threaten us with, "If you don't stop crying I'll give you something to cry about." So we stifle our feelings, swallow our pain, and hide every hurt until the pain that's afflicted us is no longer accessible to our conscious memory.

Yet that pain doesn't go away, it recedes into that dark corner of the soul called the unconscious. The pain is buried so deep that we don't even know it's there, and we deeply resent anyone who threatens to expose it.

The hidden heart is like a basement into which we throw all the trash we don't know how else to dispose of. Even religion, distorting certain Bible verses, often teaches us to place the past behind us and quickly forget about it [5].

That's good advice if the pain has been resolved, but if it hasn't we're just throwing more putrid, emotional trash in our basement. Eventually the stench will permeate our living room (and maybe even the bedroom!). Some of us are so afraid of these feelings that we lock the cellar door, put a rug over it, a table on top of it, and hope no one ever finds out it's there.

The problem is that if the pain is not really dead, the past doesn't stay buried. It's like a visceral Freddie Kruger, eternally erupting from the grave in one form or another to stalk and torment us.

Unhealed pain makes us sabotage our own best interests, making it impossible to raise our self- esteem, conquer fears, overcome our besetting sins, or deal with many dilemmas that keep us in our ruts. And, as my spiritual father Warren Campbell used to say, a rut is just a grave with the ends knocked out.

So what's the solution? You can heal anything you can feel. To heal these hurts we must reconnect with them. They must be allowed up into the living room of our conscious awareness. We must be willing to relive the hurts, in order to properly resolve them. We must re-experience the pain and, with God's help, fully feel it, heal it, and deal with the residue that was left from the original event.

Then, and only then, can we be truly healed, then, and only then, can we be freed from the pain that binds us.

The pain may take many forms. What I am calling pain may

be depression, loneliness, fear, anguish, guilt, hatred, remorse, emptiness, shame, worthlessness, humiliation, or any other negative emotion you can think of.

Whatever your pain is, once it's properly encountered and after it's appropriately resolved, healing takes place.

When the pain is gone the painkiller is no longer necessary. The sins you indulged in to dull the pain, the longings that were shortening your life, no longer have any power over you. You are free from their dominion forever.

Sounds too good to be true, but it isn't. I'll share with you the simple techniques that we use in our retreats to bring unhealed pain to the surface for healing. First though, there are some more things I need you to think about.

SCRIPTURE TO MEDITATE ON THIS WEEK:

"For what I am doing, I do not understand. For what I will to do, that I do not practice; but what I hate, that I do. ... It is no longer I who do it, but sin that dwells in me; ... Who will deliver me from this body of death? I thank God through Jesus Christ our Lord. ... There is therefore no condemnation to those who are in Christ Jesus, who do not walk according to the flesh, but according to the Spirit. For the law of the Spirit of life in Christ Jesus made me free from the law of sin and death." (Romans 7:15, 17; 8:1-2)

FOOTNOTES:

[1] Revelations 20:12

[2] Mark 7:15-23

[3] Romans 7:20

[4] Romans 7:15-16

[5] II Corinthians 5:17

JOURNALING QUESTIONS:

1. How do you handle anger? Do you stuff it, cry, or rage out of control?

_____

_____

_____

_____

_____

2. Are you overweight? Many people use food to fill the emptiness and dull their pain. Have you ever felt that you may have an eating disorder? If so what? Does food have power over you? Do you eat to live or live to eat?

_____

_____

_____

_____

_____

3. Do you have any problem with abusing alcohol, or illicit or prescription drugs?

_____

_____

_____

_____

_____

4. Is sex a problem for you? In what way? How about destructive relationships?

_____

_____

_____

_____

_____

5. What about work, talking, rage, or religion? Is there any way in which you could be considered a work addict, talkaholic, rageaholic, or addicted to religion or self-righteousness?

_____

_____

_____

_____

_____

6. When did you start having problems in any of the above areas? At what age did you start acting out sexually or abusing food, drugs, work, or anything else mentioned in this section? What was going on in your life at that time?

_____

_____

_____

_____

_____

CHAPTER 10

TECHNIQUES FOR HEALING EMOTIONAL PAIN

W HEN I FIRST STARTED DOING this ministry it was because a person in our church had come to me for help. She had tried Bible study, scripture memorization, worship, home group attendance, inner healing, counseling, and even deliverance from evil spirits, but nothing solved her problem. She kept having trouble in relationships, especially with men.

I too was frustrated. I had read about the promises in the Bible to heal the broken-hearted. I had done everything I could to find the healing I needed, and help my parishioners and counselees do the same, but they, and I, needed more.

In my search for more, I had read the writings of Cecil Osborne. A conservative Baptist pastor for over thirty years, he had earned a Ph.D. in psychology through his search for answers to the human dilemma.

Then he stumbled onto some techniques that offered his

patients dramatic breakthroughs. He explains this in his book, *Understanding Your Past, The Key to Your Future.*

I eventually flew to San Francisco to spend a week with Dr. Osborne and his wife so I could heal more of my own pain and learn about his techniques. When this woman came to me, I decided to incorporate Dr. Osborne's theories, with some of my own, about spiritual gifts in small groups to see if I couldn't help her more. She was glad to be a guinea pig. "Anything that can help," she gamely volunteered.

The techniques we used were more effective than anything I could have imagined. When she first came to me, she had no memories before the age of 13. But in three sessions with a home group in our church we saw the core problems she was dealing with emerge from the basement of her soul, where they had been suppressed and buried for more than twenty years.

We made more progress in three weeks than traditional counselors usually achieve in three years. She received healing and resolution for things that had plagued her from her earliest childhood, things that had led to a pre-marital pregnancy, a divorce, numerous heartbreaks, and countless other fractured relationships.

The techniques we used were remarkably simple. Some required the active participation of a small group, some could be done alone. None required medication, advanced academic degrees, or sophisticated psychological knowledge. Let me share with you the simple methods that have since made a profound difference in literally thousands of lives.

1. The best position for receiving healing ministry is horizontal. It's important when a person is receiving healing ministry that they recline in a prone position. The reason is very simple. As I've said, you can't heal what you can't feel, and it's simply easier to access your feelings when you're lying on your back.

However, healing ministry can be done when a person is vertical, sitting or standing (And it should be done this way if the person is a victim of rape or incest or has trust issues that would interfere with them being able to receive healing ministry if they were lying down).

Yet this does complicate things. Imagine having dental work or surgery done while standing or sitting. You could do it, but it would make it that much harder.

When I was conducting a seminar on this, a woman helped me see why lying down is more effective. She told us that she was a voice major in college. Every time they were to learn a new song her voice teacher made the whole choir lay down, so they could breathe more effectively, be less conscious of their bodies, and feel the music more intimately. This is why it works in healing ministry as well. Being in a prone position causes emotions to surface and be easily felt.

The phenomenon known as being slain in the Spirit, or literally knocked off of one's feet through an encounter with the Lord's presence, is quite commonplace now but I have my own theory about that. I think the Lord lays us down so we can better receive ministry. For emotional issues, it should be when ministry begins, not when it ends.

2. Deep breathing is essential. Breathing is very important. In the original Greek, breath and spirit are the same word. Jesus breathed on people to enable them to receive the Holy Spirit [1].

Man was made in God's image when the Lord's breath came into contact with clay. It created the soul [2], that uniquely human facet of our personality.

In our culture we've been conditioned to breathe shallowly. This helps us suppress our pain. In the healing ministry we want the pain to surface, so we encourage people to breathe deeply, perhaps more deeply than they ever have. This brings feelings to the surface, feelings that have been suppressed for many years.

At our advanced healing retreats, we get people breathing deeply from the first day. Within the first twenty-four hours, most people receive more healing than they have through any event they have ever tried.

3. Keep your mouth open. We also ask people to keep their mouth slightly open. This helps keep them from swallowing or stifling the feelings that surface.

4. Touch is very important, but it must be done judiciously. We found that in the healing ministry everything must be done with a delicate sensitivity to the Holy Spirit's leading. Often this means doing the opposite of what comes naturally. What I mean is this. If you care about people and want to help them, you may find in this ministry that the very compassion you feel will get in the way. In Joan's case, when deep, traumatic, painful feelings started to surface we all wanted to comfort her. Some of us wanted to just rub her arm, hold her, or wipe away her tears, but the Holy Spirit showed me that would not help. She needed to fully feel her pain.

Many of the things we were inclined to do would have lifted her right out of the very feelings she needed to experience in order to find the underlying cause of her hurt and sorrow.

Later, when the time was right and she had gotten through her pain, our hugs and embraces were very important. In fact I've seen people healed by the right kind of hug given at the right time. Yet, if done too soon, it can hurt more than help.

5. Look for appropriate localization of feelings. When we don't cognitively know what needs to be healed we can often find it with our heart. Pain is stored in our bodies. If we don't know what's wrong with us, we can ask God to show us and He will give us remarkable clues.

An example of this surfaced when I was conducting a seminar in Columbus, Ohio some years ago. I said that feelings in our body could show us blocked emotions that needed healing. A young man said that as I talked, he felt pain in his legs and he wondered what it meant.

I prayed for wisdom and said, "Well, I don't know you and I can't see how tall you are because you are sitting down but I would suggest that leg pain could mean that you are not as tall as you'd like to be. Also, maybe you can't run as fast as you want, and those things may have been a source of pain for you when you were growing up." He immediately said, "Bingo on both counts," and received healing ministry for the pain his short legs had caused him.

Part of the healing, as strange as this may sound, was for him to ask his legs to forgive him for the way in which he had judged them, and to thank God that his legs had always been healthy. I think if he hadn't healed that pain, he could have developed leg problems later in life. Fortunately, we'll never know.

Under this category, we find that headaches during healing ministry are usually a sign that the person is trying to do with their head what they need to do with their feelings. They're trying to figure out their pain instead of feel it out. Backaches are often a sign that a person is carrying too heavy a load in life.

Chest pain can literally be a sign of an unhealed, broken heart. Each of these things can also mean something very different altogether. Whatever pain surfaces, the best way to heal it is to fully feel it, and to express through groans, shouts, crying, or screaming anything that is necessary to get the pain fully to the surface.

Ironically, this is a pain that people often say feels good because on the other side of the pain, healing prayer can, and often does, enable the person to feel better than they've ever felt in their life.

SCRIPTURE TO MEDITATE ON THIS WEEK:

"And the Lord God formed the man of the dust of the ground, and breathed into his nostrils the breath of life; and man became a living being." (Genesis 2:7)

Jesus "Breathed on them, and said to them, 'Receive the Holy Spirit.'" (John 20:22)

FOOTNOTES:

[7] John 20:22

[8] Genesis 2:7

EXERCISE AND JOURNALING QUESTIONS:

1. Get totally alone, where no one can hear you, and any phone or doorbell can't interrupt you. Close your eyes, lie flat on your back, and pray for the Lord to show you any areas of your life that He wants to heal. Now breathe deeply, as deep as you can, three times. Expel each breath as thoroughly as you can from your lungs.

   Keep your mouth open and be aware of any part of your body that hurts or otherwise feels uncomfortable. Give yourself at least five minutes for these feelings to surface. When they do, resist the temptation to push them back down or analyze them.

   Get out of your head as much as you can. Then fully feel and let those feelings be expressed in whatever way you want. Take as much time as you want for this. Don't rush it.

2. What feelings surfaced? What do they mean to you?

   What memories, if any, did this trigger for you? Finish these sentences by letting your pen just flow freely. Don't think about your answer, just let it tumble from your pen: Lord, when I asked you to show me something just now I felt:

   _____

   _____

   _____

   _____

   _____

I think this is because:

_____

_____

_____

_____

_____

Lord, I wish You would:

_____

_____

_____

_____

_____

End this exercise by praying, "Lord, heal the hurts that underlie these feelings, in your time and way. Show me whatever I need to understand in order to complete my healing in this area of my life. Thank you, in Jesus name, Amen." (Again if you want to know why we pray in Jesus' name, read Chapter 16 next.)

CHAPTER 11

METHODS FOR HEALING THE PAIN THAT BINDS YOU

HEALING IS WITHIN YOUR GRASP. You don't need a miracle working evangelist or some weird, existential religious experience. God doesn't need to turn you into a barking cow or a clucking chicken in public.

Interestingly, properly trained lay people can make marvelous healers. Over and over we've seen wonderful results, using small groups of gifted, caring people to minister healing to one another.

And the beat goes on, long after we leave. One church, in the wake of one of our seminars, had seventy small groups continue an on-going ministry to one another. Last I knew, that continued more than a year later with dramatic healings taking place each week.

This kind of ministry won't somehow harm your church, as some pastors' fear. Quite the contrary, a number of churches that have sponsored our seminars have spontaneously doubled in size within a year. None have experienced problems with introspection, or people being harmed in some way. All reported that it was one of the most positive things they have ever done for their people. One pastor told us that the healing seminar we led for his church was changing his entire city.

People got up from their healing experience and went across town to seek forgiveness for those they had wronged. His church doubled in three months and members of 30 other churches attended weekly meeting to learn how to receive and share healing using our techniques.

How does this happen? Being transparent, admitting our own need for care and ministry enables some extraordinary things to happen. People learn what makes others the way they are and that releases mercy instead of judgment.

As we accept each other in our vulnerability, love and compassion flow, enabling people to care for one another in a warm, powerful, healing fashion. In other words, Jesus shows up in and through His people!

I'm going to teach you what I have taught others about ministering to one another. You may want to gather a small group of friends to learn this with you. If so, each will probably want their own workbook.

The exercise at the end of this chapter will enable you to form a small group to help you with your healing journey should you desire to try it.

In healing ministry like this I've learned that there are certain verbal and spiritual methods that are important.

We must do things differently than we would in traditional talk therapy.

1. First it's important not to talk too much. We all have a tendency to be uncomfortable with silence. This is counter-productive in healing ministry. When a person is receiving healing ministry you don't know what's going through their head. Your talking could short-circuit strong feelings that are beginning to surface.

I had a man come to me for healing once who lay on the floor of my office for two and a half hours without saying hardly a word. I disciplined myself to remain quiet and just pray for him. He began to groan. His whole body contorted as he writhed in pain on my office floor.

At certain points he shouted out his feelings of rage, and cried out the deep pain that surfaced. Later, he laughed exuberantly, experiencing an enormous range of powerful, healing feelings. I was often tempted to ask how he was doing or what he was feeling, but my purpose was to help him, not to satisfy my own curiosity.

When he was done, he told me what he had heard and seen on the "split screen" of his mind (By that I mean while he was reliving certain things from his past he was also conscious of being present in my office).

He had seen his grandfather demean his father when his dad was a little boy, long before he was born. He saw how this wounded his father, how it devastated him. That insight gave him grace for his father that he had never been able to have before. It released him from untold suffering just finding compassion for his father like that.

We might wonder how a man could "see" such a thing, but the God who transcends time and space knew us before He founded the earth [1]. He certainly knows everything that made us the way we are. That's why He can have such profound compassion for us [2]. When a revelation like that can help us He freely gives it.

You can see that if I had talked when I felt like it, it would have short-circuited those feelings, and he probably wouldn't have received the tremendous healing he had that day. Always err on the side of saying too little, rather than too much.

2. Secondly, be entirely open to whatever the person needs to say or express. Don't edit what the person says or their attitudes. Encourage the person who's receiving ministry to do the same. What I mean is that it's not helpful to say, "You shouldn't feel that way."

Feelings are morally neutral. They must be openly felt, whatever they are. Most of us have spent our entire lives having someone judge or criticize our feelings.

The same is true for their verbalizations. I hate swearing. Our whole culture is saturated with far too much of it, but sometimes the only way to express something awful is with the judicious use of profanities. It may be the only way the person can get out what their feeling.

At that time, your acceptance of them helps to validate the awful feelings they're having and tells them that the Lord is more concerned about them and the pain they've had, than He is about relatively trivial matters of personal behavior.

I heard about a pastor who stood before his congregation and gave this short sermon. "Point one: one third of the people in a certain country in Africa are dying of starvation. Point two: most of you don't give a damn. Point three: some of you are more offended that I said damn than you are that one third of these people are starving to death." He then sat down. The stunning sermon was over.

Often Christians give the impression that we care more about matters of propriety than we do about matters if pivotal importance. Giving people permission to speak and feel in an unedited fashion communicates to the person receiving healing the opposite. God cares deeply about them and their pain.

I was surprised to learn that the word nice does not appear even once in the Bible, yet it's the very essence of some people's definition of what it means to be a Christian. Jesus wasn't always nice and we shouldn't necessarily be either.

3. Use open-ended questions. It's said in counseling that we're only as good as our last question. An open-ended question is a question that can't be answered with yes or no. Asking someone open ended questions forces a person to think and talk, to express how they really feel.

Instead of saying, "Does that hurt?" for instance, you might ask, "What does that feel like?"

One of the most poignant questions I've heard is, "Why do you laugh when you're hurting?" We've all learned to do this, but having someone call us on it can really help us reconnect with suppressed feelings.

4. Probably the single most powerful tool we've found in helping someone deal with their pain is having them talk to the person who hurt them. This can even be done if that person is dead.

Don't read too much into this. I'm not talking about actually communicating with the dead. That's seriously forbidden behavior and can be dangerous [1]. I'm merely advocating some helpful role-playing.

Many people who are physically dead can still be very alive for us emotionally. When I went on an intensive two week healing retreat, I was coached into using a form of role playing with my dead father's image that helped free me from a self-hatred that I had dealt with for my entire Christian life.

Afterwards, as I debriefed that experience with the therapist, he explained that it wasn't my actual father I was dealing with but his imago, the image I bore of him within my soul.

We all bear the images of our parents, living and dead, and many other people deep within us. Some people think that each marriage bed also contains both the husband's and wife's father and mother, and maybe some other people as well. It can get pretty crowded! No wonder marital bliss is so elusive.

Many of our core issues result from hurt or neglect we experienced at the hands of our parents. Often, we will ask a person who is receiving healing ministry to close their eyes and talk to their parents as if they were in the room. Instead of them saying my mother used to beat me, we'll have them say, "Mommy, why did you beat me?"

The use of the word mommy instead of mother is important. It's often very difficult for a person to say, because mother hasn't been mommy for a long, long time, but talking to mommy can force painful feelings to the surface.

In a rural church where we did a seminar, my wife tried to help a man connect with his deep feelings of rage and hurt. She prompted him to say daddy. He denied that there was a problem with daddy. Denial isn't a river in Egypt; it's a pain-filled reality in the church. Despite his denial she felt impressed to probe him to try and say daddy.

Suddenly he grimaced and shouted, "DADDY-Y- Y-Y," at the top of his lungs. It almost blew the roof off of the church. Just saying daddy brought up years worth of suppressed painful memories that then could be healed and resolved.

Many people think that in facing the pain their parents have caused they are somehow dishonoring their parents.

I believe very strongly that people can do this without dishonoring them.

It's important to realize that the purpose of this is not to place blame. No one had perfect parents. Jesus is the only One who ever had a perfect Father, and He led him to an unjust, agonizing death on a cross. Jesus probably felt confused, abused, and neglected when His Father made Him accept the punishment for our sins.

When He felt that way, He didn't stifle His feelings. He openly asked His Father "Why have you forsaken me?"[1]. We can also admit our fears, disappointments, and hurts without dishonoring our parents. In fact, it may be the only way to figure out how to live honorably.

5. Spiritual and emotional techniques are also essential, especially the right kind of prayer. Later, I will share with you a particular prayer, one which we've found extremely helpful. There's nothing magical about it. You may be able to design one you like better.

Such a prayer should include praying for all feelings, memories, and experiences to surface that are essential to the healing that the Lord wants to perform. It should also include a prayer for God's love to protect from any evil or deception.

6. Then pray for current resolution of the core problem.

Often the issues that trip our hot buttons are symptomatic of deeper issues. Like a bruise on the arm that is hurt when someone bumps us, these bruises on the soul can make us hypersensitive to certain things.

The good news is that even when we can't remember the initial events, if we pay attention to our feelings, we can reopen old areas that have been shut off to our conscious memories. By riding those feelings back through time we can reconnect with things we no longer consciously remember. Such prayer can then open up old wounds for the Lord to cleanse, heal, and resolve.

7. When you hit a road block, the people praying for you can stop and ask the Lord for wisdom. At this time, if a thought, image, or impression comes to one of them, they can share it with you. It may be something like, I see a yellow house, or, does the name John mean anything to you?

These things may or may not mean anything. Any thoughts like this should be offered as non-coercively as possible. They are suggestions, never to be imposed as definite revelations or insights. If they are valid, the person receiving insight may or may not recognize it. They may also be inaccurate, so any such suggestions should be offered humbly.

When the ministry time is done, the people helping you should ask questions like, "how are you doing?" "who do you need to forgive?," and any other questions that are relevant to your healing.

Also realize that whatever happens, it's another step in your healing path, and probably not the final one. Healing and becoming whole is a heroic lifetime journey.

SCRIPTURE TO MEDITATE ON THIS WEEK:

"Come now, let us reason together," says the Lord. "Though your sins are scarlet, they shall be as white as snow. ... If you are willing and obedient, you shall eat the good of the land." (Isaiah 1:18a-19a)

FOOTNOTES:

[1] Ephesians 1:4

[2] Psalm 103:13

[3] Matthew 27:46

[4] Deuteronomy 18:10-12

EXERCISE:

For this exercise you will need a small group of trusted friends to help you.

1. Think of a problem you are facing that really trips your hot button. It could be a problem with a friend, mate, significant other, parent, child, neighbor, or someone you work with. It should involve a current situation that you feel strongly about and would like to resolve. State briefly what's going on and who it involves?

_____

_____

_____

_____

_____

2. Pick a trusted friend or small group of friends who are interested in healing ministry. It could be a home group from your church, some Christian friends in your neighborhood, people who share your interest in healing, or another area of close relationships, but it must be people who care about you and are spiritually gifted and trust-worthy. Who would you most like to have help you with this?

_____

_____

_____

_____

_____

3. It's most helpful to get them their own workbook. But you can also just have them read over this chapter (but not your description of the problem). Then have them pray the following prayer with you. When they do, have them talk and pray you through the feelings that surface:

SUGGESTED PRAYER:

"Dear Father in Heaven, Please let (say the name) feel, remember, and experience everything necessary to receive the healing that You have for him/her today. Let Your love fill, surround, and protect him/her. Holy Spirit, come with power to heal him/her and grace us with the spiritual gifts, wisdom, and insight we need to be Your healing instruments. In Jesus' name we thank You, Amen."

(If necessary, have them read Chapter 16 of the workbook to understand why we recommend you pray in Jesus' name.)

4. When your friends are prepped and ready, lie on the floor, close your eyes, and take some deep cleansing breaths to relax. Then begin telling them about the problem with which you need help. If strong emotions surface let them be fully felt and expressed. Then ride those strong feelings back through time and be aware of any memories that are triggered by the feelings.

   You very well may reconnect with a powerful memory from your past that is linked to this current situation and is the real reason why it is causing you so much anguish. If so, feel the feelings associated with that experience. Ask the Lord to take you fully through the feelings and to heal any emotions that were damaged at that time.

5. When you feel done with this experience, tell the others in the group whatever you can share about it. Then, as soon as you can, fully explain, in writing, this experience. Ask the Lord to continue healing you of the effects of it, and to show you how to sincerely forgive anyone you need to forgive for the situation. If this is hard, don't press it. There will be more about forgiveness in the next chapter, and it won't be what you expect.

CHAPTER 12

PREMATURE FORGIVENESS

THOSE OF US WHO HAVE been exposed to Christianity often feel that there are certain things we should never do, like get angry, hate, or fail to forgive. Dictums like this can clog up our entire spiritual life. To get healthy, most of us need to re-examine them in the light of the scriptures.

Most of the unspoken rules we live by in this regard are based on half- truths, which means they're also half false.

First, let's look at anger.

Many people see Christians as being passive- aggressive, hypocritical wimps. How we, as Christians, understand anger has a lot to do with this.

We may know that the Bible doesn't categorically condemn anger and that it actually says, be angry but sin not. However, most Christians I know still feel extremely guilty if they ever feel or express anger. Their inner Bible says "Never be angry or you aren't a good Christian, and anyone else who expresses anger is a bad person."

In fact, anger is dangerous. This is because it's such a powerful emotion and can easily lead us to sin. When it's not handled properly it can even shorten our life. Recent studies show that those who totally bury their anger and those who thoroughly indulge it are in danger of heart attacks. In other words both fight and flight are unhealthy. Neither blowing up nor shutting up are good for us.

Only those who appropriately handle anger will enjoy lasting health. For most of us, we must go through some transforming experiences to learn to do this.

Anger was a real problem for me. My father was a rageaholic. He never disciplined me except in anger, and that was a daily occurrence for him. As a young man, I was well on my way to being like him when I finally said and did enough things in anger to hurt those I love; I vowed to never become angry.

That's when the shut up-blow up syndrome started. I'd shut up until I blew up, all of which only compounded my guilt and further fueled my self-hatred and rage.

When I went through my mid-life crisis, I confronted my rage in a whole new way. I attended a healing retreat in a monastery in Nebraska to face and understand my issues and in a small group. We were asked to share our childhood experiences.

When I shared mine, the members of my small group made me face the fact that I was a victim of emotional rape. When my father forced me to stuff all my rage by refusing to allow me to protest his unjust treatment of me, I was violated at the core of my being.

This was a shocking revelation for me. I had worked with rape and incest victims. I knew how they had been damaged by their perpetrators, how it affected their whole lives until they got healed, but I never saw my own trauma as being in the same category.

I suppressed my rage so much I would be angry at a hundred encounters a week for someone doing a poor job, having a bad attitude, or just generally trying to rip me off, but I wouldn't tell those people about it. They ranged from the bank teller, to the guy at the gas station, to people in my church, traffic, family, and neighborhood.

I'd shut up around them and blow up at home. I'd take all their garbage, store it up with mine, and then dump it in my own living room. Sound familiar? You may know someone who does this as well.

In Nebraska, I received some deep healing ministry over these issues. I also realized I had to learn to find my voice. I had to speak up for myself. Though my father, who died in 1979, was no longer around to say, "Don't you talk back to me," my inner father was forcing me to obey his frustrating mandates.

It cost me a lot to find my voice. I lost two-thirds of my church and even a few friends, but it was well worth it. The people who left our church, and even the friends who bailed out on me, were largely toxic people. Only the ones who weren't toxic remained in my life.

When I first wrote this story I was at the smallest and best church I've ever pastored. The people there were striving to get healthy, and succeeding at it. And they gave me the grace and compassion I needed to get better as well.

My family was eventually much happier, too. Instead of manipulating them, I could speak directly to them about my concerns and they could do the same with me. This is how families and churches are supposed to function.

The no-talk rule is no longer in effect. The family secrets are out of the bag, and all of us are learning to say what we mean and mean what we say, without being mean about it!

Churches, businesses, and other organizations that fail to achieve this become extended, dysfunctional families.

Jesus didn't always hide his anger. He freely expressed his anger not only to the Pharisees but also to His disciples when they let Him down. In so doing, he released them, and us, to also be angry and sin not. Jesus didn't die to make us all a bunch of phony, secretly hostile pansies.

I believe that only those who are truly themselves can truly do the Father's business. Without coming to that place of profound self-acceptance, we will always feel as if the Lord secretly hates us. Without that, unconditional love is just another empty phrase.

Hatred is something else we think we should never harbor. In reality, there are some things we should hate, like sin for instance, and Satan. My work with satanic ritual abuse victims has taught me a healthy hatred for Satan.

We should hate the evil around us and be motivated by that hatred to do something about it. Obviously, hating the sin doesn't give us license to hate the sinner.

Hatred, like anger, is a powerful negative emotion. When properly channeled, it gives us energy for action, energy which God can use to advance His Kingdom and teach us to battle evil on His behalf. By the way, you must become healthy to be able to battle evil [1].

I'm convinced that's why there is so much spiritual resistance to the healing ministry. When people get healthy, the reign of evil is seriously threatened.

Finally, one of the key things that holds us back is a misunderstanding about forgiveness. It's what I call premature forgiveness.

We all know we're to forgive those who have wronged us. But I've seldom heard forgiveness taught the way Jesus taught it. He said, unless we forgive from the heart we won't be forgiven, [2] and there's the rub.

True forgiveness is more than a simple act of the will.

It's a heartfelt release of our judgments against another, and that's much more complicated.

When I became aware of my lingering anger with my father, I prayed for wisdom about how to handle it. Even though he had given his life to the Lord and mellowed out late in life (as many men do when their testosterone subsides), there was still some antagonism between us.

I had heard that the earliest memory a person has can reveal a lot about them, so in an attempt to understand him better I asked my father about his earliest memory. I'll never forget his answer.

He said, "I remember looking up and seeing three lights over my head." When I asked him what they were he said, very matter-of-factly, "I was eighteen months old and I had been hospitalized because my bowels had fallen out due to malnutrition."

I was stunned. I didn't know what to say. Like most of our parents, he had done his crummy best. I had never known hunger a day in my life. My father had succeeded in giving me what he never had, plenty of food on my plate and a roof over my head. He hadn't even had that.

My relationship with my father still had its rough spots, but that day, my anger with him was largely defused. I never felt the same anger towards him after that. I released my judgments against him and realized it was a miracle that he had never been worse than he was.

There's an Arabian proverb that says, "To know all is to forgive all." It's very true. God can forgive anything because He knows everything that made us the way we are, which is why He encourages us to pray for those who hurt and use us [3].

I don't think we're supposed to pray that those people change, but rather that we see them as God does. For through his eyes, we all need grace. A funny and wonderful thing happens if you'll do that.

When we stop judging people it releases something in them that enables them to change. Unforgiveness is one of the terrible ways we bind people on earth. Heartfelt forgiveness is one of the marvelous ways we can set them free.

If you're having a hard time forgiving, relax. Ask the Lord for help. Pray for wisdom, work on healing your own pain, and ask Him to enable you to release your judgments. If necessary, talk through the issues with the people who have wronged you. [4]. One way or another you'll eventually be able to forgive them from the heart.

How do you know when you've done that? If you find yourself saying, 'I forgive you but I never want to see you again,' you haven't done it yet. Forgiveness is only real when you can sincerely wish the person well who has harmed you. When you can truly bless those who have cursed you, then you will both be free.

It's easy to lay a guilt trip on people about forgiveness. It's easy for me to tell you that you should forgive. But knowing what you should do and being able to do it are two different things.

With God's help, we can genuinely forgive and be free of our bitterness and resentment. That's marvelous news, for nothing else clogs our spiritual arteries as badly as unforgiveness. When we're free of the blockage, few things have the capacity to make us happier and healthier.

SCRIPTURE TO MEDITATE ON THIS WEEK:

"You have heard that it was said, 'You shall love your neighbor and hate your enemy,' but I say to you, love your enemies, bless those who curse you, and pray for those who spitefully use you and persecute you, that you may be sons of your Father in Heaven; for He makes His sun rise on the evil and the good, and sends rain on the just and the unjust. For if you love those who love you, what reward have you? Do not even tax gatherers do the same? And if you greet your brethren only, what do you do more than others? Do not even tax collectors do so? Therefore you shall be perfect, just as your Father in Heaven is perfect." (Matthew 5:43-48)

FOOTNOTES:

[1] Malachi 4:1-3

[2] Matthew 6:15, 18:35

[3] Matthew 5:44

[4] Matthew 18:15

JOURNALING QUESTIONS:

1. Who do you have a hard time forgiving from the heart?

_____

_____

_____

_____

_____

2. What did they do to you?

_____

_____

_____

_____

_____

3. How is it affecting you?

_____

_____

_____

_____

_____

4. Write a letter you will not send. Freely express everything you feel about this situation and the people involved. Then

ask the Lord to show you anything you need to see, or do, to be able to forgive from the heart. When you are finished with this you may want to seek healing ministry for the pain the situation caused you.

CHAPTER 13

THE ONE THING THAT CAN KEEP YOU BOUND

THERE IS SO MUCH EMPHASIS today on self-esteem, and free-ing ourselves from guilt, and so little of it is working. We realize our guilt is killing us, that the worse we feel about ourselves the worse we behave and the worse our lives become, but we don't know what to do about it. We don't know how to end the downward spiral of sin, guilt, low self-esteem, and further depravity.

Part of the problem, as I said in my book, *True Sexuality*, is that we have failed to realize that all guilt is not psychological. There is such a thing as true moral guilt. Some things like child rape are universally wrong.

When we violate those things, though our mind may rationalize our behavior, our heart betrays us. Deep down we know we've done wrong. The guilt we feel about ourselves in our heart of hearts can keep us tightly bound.

No matter how callous we've become, every time we do wrong, it robs us of a piece of ourselves.

It diminishes the way we feel about ourselves in our own eyes, and eventually in the eyes of others as well. While a low self-concept can keep us bound; we ultimately need healing to become truly free. Unfortunately, even the most effective small groups in the United States have missed this essential point.

Twelve step groups have been very good at helping people face their own reality. They've helped millions come out of denial, self-pity, victimization, and accept responsibility for their lives. The one thing these groups can't do is truly heal the pain that binds us.

For that to happen we need a different form of divine intervention. As I've pointed out, we don't just need a vague higher power, we need for the Highest Power's healing to be released for us through the Holy Spirit, working through other gifted healers [1].

This is God's way to heal the broken-hearted and set the captives free. But even people who know they need this healing sometimes find it to be an elusive thing. Here's why.

In the religious community, we have emphasized forgiveness to the point that we sometimes think that it's all the healing the Lord has for us. However, while forgiveness is good, it alone can't heal.

If I accidentally step on your toe and break it, then turn and ask you to forgive me, you won't be instantly healed just because you release your judgment against me. To be sure, forgiving me can keep you from being infected with bitterness and resentment, it can keep you from getting worse, but it won't heal you.

Forgiveness cleans the wound, it keeps us from becoming bitter, but it takes real healing to make us completely better.

When we began to do small group healing work I noticed a fascinating phenomenon. I can only describe it this way, when we would get a person in touch with the original pain that was binding them; there was inevitably a form of spiritual infection inhibiting the healing process.

It was the same for every person. Every time we opened an old wound, a form of spiritual puss drained out.

It was exactly what the Bible said would be there. It was the remnants of unhealed emotional pain. I am talking about hidden hatred, a hatred that can be directed at others, but which is more likely to be directed inward at oneself. Unless it's dealt with, unless it's truly removed, it spreads like a spiritual cancer and soon destroys the very cells of one's soul.

This isn't some spooky New Age theory. Even the Ten Commandments discuss it. In Exodus 20, we are told that the sins of the fathers are visited on the third and fourth generation of those who hate God.

People call this generational sin, but few of the people I've heard speak about it seem to really understand it. Most people act as if all we need to do is repent and we'll be free of its pernicious grip. Unfortunately, it's not that easy.

Someone once said that for every complicated problem there's a simple answer that's wrong. This is a classic case of that.

I was recently consulting a case of a man who has some severe problems. The woman who was trying to help him had observed an amazing thing. Even though this fellow hardly knew his father, he was becoming exactly like him. In fact, he was manifesting precisely the same destructive behavior his father had.

This is what I'm talking about. In our generation, so many people are conscious of their parent's shortcomings, and trying so hard to avoid making their mistakes, that it's ironic how many people come to me with the same complaint.

Despite their best efforts, they are becoming exactly like their parents. Their personal history is repeating itself and they are making the very same mistakes that their parents did.

The reason for this is simple. The Bible's warned us about it for thousands of years. Wherever there's hatred in our heart, we'll be visited by generational sin. The sins of our fathers, grandfathers, and even great-great grandfathers will become our sins. We will inevitably reap the consequences of their rebellion and shortcomings.

When I first stumbled upon this, a nurse in our church explained it to me in medical terms. She likened the experience to a sterile abscess. A sterile abscess is a wound that was cleaned and closed but the underlying tissue didn't heal. This can lead to gangrene.

The same thing happens to the soul. If a person's been wounded and they have forgiven the person who wounded them but never healed the damage that was done, the wound becomes infected.

The spiritual puss that infects emotional wounds is hatred towards God.

I call this hidden hatred because it can be very subtle and hard to detect. *That's because hatred is not the opposite of love.*

Many people think they couldn't possibly hate God because they love Him. But you can love and hate the same person. In fact, *hatred is love gone sour.* You can only hate someone you once loved, and this can happen very quickly.

The classic example of this is the young girl who was victimized by incest. Each night when her father came into her room to molest her, she cried out to God to protect her. Each time He seemed to fail her.

Night after night, her father continued his insidious assault on her very being. She finally concluded that God didn't care about her. If He did, He surely would have rescued her.

Later in life, she may give her life to the Lord and be born again. While she appreciates the great gift of abundant and eternal life, she may find herself restrained in her affections towards God and men. She loves God, but she can't fully trust Him.

He seems like one more man who only wants something from her. So even though she may dutifully serve Him, she may find it impossible to really love Him.

As her relationships with men and others suffer, and as she has trouble raising her own children, she may eventually seek healing ministry. And in the midst of reliving the awful emotional pain that's been stored in her for so many years, she may be shocked to hear herself crying out, in an unguarded moment, "I hate You, I hate You," and realize she is saying it to the Lord.

But it's okay. God has broad shoulders, He can take it. He already knows she secretly feels that way. He's just been waiting for her to acknowledge it. Then He can clarify things, and begin to heal her pain.

Then, after she's gotten the spiritual puss of hidden hatred out of her soul, and after she's emptied her heart of the spiritual garbage it's been carrying around [2], she can hear what He's wanted to say to her. It might go something like this:

"My beloved daughter, I didn't want those awful things to happen to you. I never wanted your father to do what He did to you. But I've given him freedom and I've given you freedom too. I won't turn either you or him into robots, forcing you to do things my way.

For if I did that, any affection you have for me wouldn't really be love, it would be that which comes from an automaton. I hurt when you hurt. I've yearned to be close to you and heal your pain. And if you'll let me, I'll make you better than if you'd never been wounded. For as in the physical world so it is also in the matters of the soul. Where a wound is cleansed and properly healed the tissue becomes stronger than tissue that's never been damaged.

Beyond that, if you want, I will use your experience to heal others.

I love to use wounded healers. The word of your testimony can overcome Satan and his lies in the lives of others whom he's bound. As you let me use you to share with and heal others, your healing will spring forth mightily [3], and you will find deep meaning and satisfaction in life."

Once a person hears and receives that kind of message from the Lord, they are well on their way to being fully healed of their pain.

For this healing to be completed four things must happen. First, they must re-contact the old wound. The exercises in the previous chapter show you how. Secondly, they must own and experience whatever feelings are there. Third, they must walk in the light [4].

This is best done with the elders of the church being invited for a session of mutual confession [5]. Notice it's not the pastor's job to visit the sick; it's the elders' job to heal them! Many people wonder why there isn't more healing in the church. The answer is quite simple.

If you want New Testament results, use New Testament techniques. *Most churches that believe in healing anoint with oil, as is recommended in the book of James, but few use the mutual confession of the elders, and that's what releases healing virtue.* That confessing "one to another" is the key that unlocks the Lord's power to heal. When the elders are called to confess, this creates vulnerable leadership, not shallow relationships.

While all sickness isn't related to sin, some is. Other ailments are complicated by unresolved guilt that keeps the immune system ineffective. Mutual confession allows them to explore any issues related to sin and guilt that would interrupt the flow of healing.

Finally, and only after the first three steps will they be ready to do it, they must do whatever it takes to forgive from the depths of their heart.

Properly handled, our wounds can scour away evil [6]. Mishandled or ignored, they can make us bitter, guilt-ridden, and resentful. Though we try to cover up the hatred with a veneer of religiosity, perceptive people, pets, and little children will see through it.

To be truly healed we must be open to the possibility that we may still harbor some hatred towards the Lord and others. If it's there, and we face it, we can be healed.

If we don't, we are doomed to repeat history. We will pass on our sins and pain to our children and grandchildren. And who would ever want to do that?

SCRIPTURE TO MEDITATE ON THIS WEEK:

"Is anyone among you sick? Let him call for the elders of the church, and let them pray over him, anointing him with oil in the name of the Lord. And the prayer of faith will save the sick, and the Lord will raise him up. And if he has committed sins, he will be forgiven. Confess your trespasses to one another, and pray for one another, that you may be healed. The effective, fervent prayer of a righteous man avails much." *(James 5: 13-16)*

FOOTNOTES:

[1] I Corinthians 12:9

[2] Matthew 12:34

[3] Isaiah 58:8

[4] I John 1:7

[5] James 5:13-16

[6] Proverbs 20:30

EXERCISE AND JOURNALING QUESTIONS:

1. Ask the Lord to search your heart and see if there is any evil way within you. Then be alert to anything that comes across your path in the next few days to show you the things that are wrong.

2. What have been the major hurts and disappointments in your life?

_____

_____

_____

_____

_____

3. When have you felt like the Lord let you down the most in your life?

_____

_____

_____

_____

_____

4. Write Him another letter about these incidents. Be as open as you can with Him. Tell Him exactly how you felt at the time and ask Him to forgive you, to cleanse you and to help you rebuild your trust.

5. Find another person, preferably of the same sex, with whom you can walk in the light, someone you can share anything with. If you need further healing, share James 5:13-16 with your pastor and ask him which elders you can meet with for mutual confession and healing prayer.

CHAPTER 14

REDEMPTIVE RELATIONSHIPS

THE WRONG RELATIONSHIPS CAN BE the thing that hurt us the most, but the right ones can heal us. By right ones, I don't mean relationships where there's no hurt involved. There are very few of those in life.

What I mean are relationships where we learn to handle our hurts redemptively, relationships we can use for greater self-understanding, insight, and even healing.

Usually, problems we're currently having in our relationships are not the root problems, they're just symptoms of our real issues. If we can accept this, and learn what to do about it, this will not only make every relationship in our lives better, but it will also give us the most useful tool we can have for progressing on our healing journey.

Like I said earlier, often, the things people do that hurt us are painful because we have hurt stored within us. Their actions touch our hurt, bumping up against our bruises, and compounding our pain, but they are seldom the primary source of our pain.

In our seminars, to help people understand this, I have people close their eyes and experience what they feel when I say a certain word. I then ask them to open their eyes and describe their feelings.

Though I say the same word to everyone, their feelings usually run a gamut from the very best, to the absolute worst. Some people describe incredible warmth at the mention of the word while others clench their teeth in unfeigned rage. That word is Mother.

Everyone has some experience with the concept mother, even Jesus. At one point His mother seemed to think He was crazy, and that He should just forget this healing and prophetic stuff and come back to the carpenter's shop.

Every person's experience with the concept mother is slightly different, even if they share the same mother. That's why it's essential that we own our feelings.

What I mean is this. Each of us has bruises within us related to our past. There are no exceptions, we've all been wounded. When someone comes along and trips our trigger, when they do something that pushes our hot buttons, we need to stop playing the blame game and own our feelings.

This means that when we are hurt, instead of saying, "You made me feel...," we need to learn to say, "When you did such and such, I felt ...."

Do you see the difference? In the first instance, we are accusing. We are making someone else responsible for our feelings. In doing so we are setting ourselves up for further hurt and frustration.

In the second scenario, we are accepting ownership of our

feelings, acknowledging that they're a part of us. Instead of accusing, we're revealing a part of ourselves to our loved one.

We are saying, "I care about you, and I want you to know me. You probably didn't realize it, or mean it, but when you said and did such and such, it brought these feelings to the surface in me."

Not only will this keep the person from being on the defensive, but it will also afford you the wonderful opportunity to examine the feelings you are having and, with the help of another who loves you, understand what is in your heart that may still require healing. It's a far more mature way to process your emotions, one that affords endless opportunities for growth, healing, and closer relationships.

When we walk in the light with others instead of hiding our darkest selves in secret, we have genuine fellowship [1]. And real fellowship is more than looking at the back of someone's head, or even shaking hands with strangers during a greeting time in the worship service.

Jesus modeled this by living with His disciples for over three years. That's a radical departure from the, "don't-let-anyone-get-to-know-you," school of theology. When we do healing ministry, this kind of intimacy, trust, and understanding are essential.

When someone lies on the floor, preparing to share with us their personal struggles, we use certain guidelines for conducting the initial healing interview. These guidelines can help move the person forward towards their healing.

Much of this has to do with getting them in touch with the feelings that were there before the current relational problem existed. These feelings, properly understood, will lead us to the core issues and help us find the earlier pain that needs to be healed.

You can do the same thing in exploring your own relational problems. It will help you enormously in your effort to redeem relational struggles and use them to advance your healing journey.

Foremost, listen to feelings. Someone may say, "that didn't bother me," but their feelings tell you otherwise. Learn to watch their eyes. Listen for the subtle changes in a person's voice that will tell you there is something happening contrary to what they are saying. Watch their body language. Jesus was a master at reading people's true intentions.

Pressured speech is a sure sign that something more is going on. It's that high-pitched voice we get when we're trying hard to be super nice or convince someone that something is true when it isn't.

The healthier people become, the more they can risk allowing their voice to reveal how they really feel, and the fewer games they must play to cover up strong emotions.

Whatever you do, whether you are ministering healing to someone or trying to help a loved one express their feelings, don't force things. If you create a comfortable enough environment people will open up. Coercion and manipulation are never conducive to healthy relationships, or healing.

At our retreats, I set up a banner on the first day, which sets the exact tone we want. I don't know where the quote came from, but I cherish it. (Some attribute the quote to a woman named George Sand.) It says,

"Oh the comfort, the inexpressible comfort of feeling safe with a person, having neither to weigh thoughts nor measure words - but pouring them all right out -

Just as they are - chaff and grain together, certain that

a faithful hand will take and sift them - keep what is worth keeping - and, with a breath of kindness, blow the rest away."

That kind of environment is how all of life ought to be. It's what I call the real world, how God wants the world to be. The rest of life is the unreal world. In this kind of real world, it's safe to grow, to heal, and to simply be. We can create that real world wherever we choose.

You also must become comfortable with silence. Notice how few words Jesus spoke. We're so used to filling every available moment of our lives with music, chatter, television, or something, that we often miss the opportunity that silence offers us to get in touch with who we really are and what we really feel.

I value the friends I can take a long trip with and sit in prolonged silence, comfortable just being with someone without feeling I must keep the conversational ball in the air.

Silence truly is golden. It can really help us to access our emotions, or just feel accepted by the people with whom we are silent. In healing ministry it's absolutely necessary that we embrace silence. It will yield the greatest revelations.

When in doubt, pray. If you don't know what to say, or you don't know how you feel or what you think, ask God to show you [2]. This is especially valuable in healing work. Pray for wisdom and then wait for an inspired thought.

As long as you have asked the Lord to protect you from being deceived you won't be led astray. And He will often give you divinely inspired ideas that will help you, or another person, move further along the healing path.

When you discover an old wound, certain things are extremely helpful. In this case it's important to look for core issues and key healing moments: to look for the split. What I mean is this:

In each of our lives there were moments in time when we learned, at a very early age, that being who we are isn't good enough, that we aren't acceptable the way we are.

These harsh encounters with reality may have come from parents, teachers, friends, classmates, or all of the above. They are part and parcel of the civilizing process we have all gone through. They force us to deny and split off a part of who we are.

These splits are extremely painful. They come early in life, before puberty, and often much sooner. They reveal the moments of deepest personal hurt we've encountered. And though they were important in our development, we may or may not remember them.

Part of the way we deal with pain we don't know how to heal is by forgetting about it. When discussing a relational problem, or performing healing ministry, we have unique opportunities to reconnect with those times when our personalities split off.

In an extreme form, those split off personalities become alternative identities, or alters. We see that we can't be who we are so we act like someone else. If the trauma has been exceptional, such as incest, rape, or deep abuse, a person actually feels so unsafe being who they are that they become someone else. This, in my opinion, is the origin of multiple personalities.

For most of us, this is not the case. We merely mask our feelings, hide our identity, and act like someone else to increase our chances of being accepted.

When we encounter a split, a moment when it was no longer safe to be who we are, and we have to act like someone else, those incidents are usually filled with unhealed pain. Reopening these wounds and allowing the liniment of God's love to penetrate to their depths and heal them, yields the greatest life-changing experiences people will have.

Nothing I've seen has greater power to free people from the pain that binds them to destructive behavior. Often after such healing encounters, compulsive behavior patterns simply evaporate.

This is what happens for people at our retreats and seminars. Often the things that made them become someone they aren't, are rediscovered, opened for healing, and resolved. The change that comes from such encounters is worth whatever it takes to get there. People often leave a retreat visibly looking five years younger, and living like it too.

I value such times so highly that I have traveled from one end of the country to the other attending any event I can find that will help me move further along in my healing journey. Though such things have cost me thousands of dollars, nothing has helped me more in life. Nothing is a better bargain for making my whole life better.

Healing doesn't cost, it pays.

A poem by E. E. Cummings embodies this struggle: "To be nobody but yourself in a world which is doing its best night and day to make you everybody else – means to fight the hardest battle that any human being can fight and never stop fighting."

Of course, for Christians, being our self means being Christ like, for we were made in His image, and nothing else truly reflects who we really are. That fight is even tougher, but also far more worthwhile.

SCRIPTURE TO MEDITATE ON THIS WEEK:

"God is light and in Him is no darkness at all. If we say we have fellowship with Him, and walk in darkness, we lie and do not practice the truth. But if we walk in the light as He is in the light, we have fellowship with one another and the blood of Jesus Christ His Son cleanses us from all sin. If we say we have no sin, we deceive ourselves, and the truth is not in us. If we confess our sins, He is faithful and just to forgive us our sins and to cleanse us from all unrighteousness. If we say we have not sinned, we make Him a liar, and His Word is not in us." (I John 1:1b-10)

FOOTNOTES:

[1] I John 1:5-10

[2] James 1:5

JOURNALING QUESTIONS:

1. What relationships cause you the most pain right now?

_____

_____

_____

_____

_____

2. If you were to own your feelings in each of these relationships, where do you think they are coming from? What
   hot buttons are these people pushing in you?

   _____

   _____

   _____

   _____

   _____

3. Could any of these relationships reveal a split that oc-
   curred earlier in your childhood? If so, what was that
   about?

   _____

   _____

   _____

   _____

   _____

4. What deep feelings of pain (negative emotions) are still
   lingering in that split?

   _____

   _____

   _____

   _____

   _____

5. What would you like to ask God to do for you about them?

_____

_____

_____

_____

_____

CHAPTER 15

NEW PARADIGMS
FOR THERAPY

FOR MANY YEARS, I RESISTED the notion of counseling anyone outside my church. When I began to realize that I had
a responsibility to help others and began to counsel for a fee I
was totally frustrated with many things I'd been taught about
counseling. As I implemented my own approach, I discovered I
could help people others hadn't helped.

Good therapy is worth a lot: it doesn't cost, it pays. Almost all
my clients had been to other therapists and not received all that
they needed. Their therapists, clergy, and religious counselors
had often done their best but we must face the facts.

Few schools, if any, of either ministry or counseling, teach
their counselors how to heal. I found I could help them quicker,
cheaper, and more effectively if I did a few things differently.
Besides using a healing approach, here are some of the things I
did differently that worked.

The first thing that had to go was the 50 minute hour. It's much
too strenuous on the therapist to meet a new person every hour.

I also found that it often took 40 minutes just to get started and as soon as soon as we began get somewhere it was time to quit. Besides that, it's not totally honest to charge people for an hour and give them 50 minutes.

I told people I'd rather see them less often and for longer time periods. This really worked. I seldom had a client need therapy for more than a year. In most cases we made tremendous progress in a few sessions, often enough that they didn't need me any longer.

Most clients resolved their issues and were profoundly better after just three to six sessions. And each session, whether it took 75 minutes or three hours (a rarity) was powerful and life changing.

Ask yourself this: if you are in therapy, would you rather see someone an hour a week for a year or three times for an average of two hours and get the better results? It's a no-brainer.

Some may think this would put therapists out of work. My experience was the opposite. When you really help people where others have failed the world beats a path to your door.

Referrals from satisfied clients made up most of my practice. After a while, I didn't have to advertise. I also had the energy I needed to do my job well. Once I implemented this policy of seeing people fewer times for longer sessions, burnout was no longer a problem.

I also insisted that people pay for their therapy.

I used to think people would value good advice even if it didn't cost them anything. I was wrong. Most people think free advice is worth what you pay for it. On the other hand, if someone pays me 180 dollars an hour, they're probably going to do what I suggest. And if they do that, my advice works wonders for them.

A way to help people who can't afford such rates is by creating a sliding scale, or allowing people to pay over time. But I never did someone a favor by letting them come for free. It was amazing how brilliant I became, and how effective my counsel was as soon as people paid for it.

I also gave people homework such as reading a recommended book, listening to tapes, journaling, or attending a retreat or seminar.

Therapists who attended our retreats equate the value of that long weekend to six months or a year's worth of therapy. What's that worth? Often after attending, they no longer need therapy any more.

The more I can get people to do outside of their time with me the less they need me and the more they can grow without paying me. And when people focus on resolving their own issues, educating themselves, and pursuing their healing aggressively, they get healthy much more quickly.

We simply need to rethink therapy to make it more effective for people. The better we are at helping people, the more successful we are, in all ways.

Scripture to meditate on this week:

"For unto us a Child is born, unto us a Son is given; and the government will be upon His shoulder. And His name shall be called Wonderful Counselor, Mighty God, Everlasting Father, Prince of Peace." (Isaiah 9: 6-7)

CHAPTER 16

WHO SHOULD BE YOUR HIGHER POWER?

WHO SHOULD BE YOUR HIGHER power, Mohammed? Buddha? Confucius? Should you consider Jesus? If so why? These are questions we must all eventually ask.

I could give you a trite, simplistic, religious-sounding answer to that question, but I'd never do that. Jesus wasn't religious and neither am I. In fact, religion got Jesus killed. It's still His worst enemy in our world today.

The reason Jesus is my higher power is intensely practical. After studying all the great religions and philosophies in the world none can begin to do for me what simple faith in the teachings of Jesus has. He is the only major religious figure in history who said that healing the brokenhearted was essential to His life mission.

He also came to give us an abundant life. I've said for years that if anyone has a better way to live, a simpler way to get the most out of life, I'll give up on Christ and try it. No one has even offered me anything close.

If there were no Heaven or Hell I'd still be a Christian. That's because scriptural Christianity has the best agenda for a rich, full, happy and meaningful life on earth. Neither Confucius, nor Buddha, nor Mohammed, nor Lao Tzu, nor any other figure in human history can do for you what Jesus can. None of them even claim to be still alive.

You might well ask, "What has Jesus done for me?" He has healed my mind, given me an exciting purpose for my life, provided me with a wonderful family, and given me terrific friends.

He's also taught me how to prosper and be in complete health, freed me from destructive compulsions, and He's in the process of restoring my bruised and wounded soul. In addition to that He's taught me how to find love, peace of mind, joy, and many other virtues that almost guarantee my life will continue on an upward spiral of fulfillment and happiness. Finally, He's promised the best eternal retirement benefits of any religion known to man.

I used to be an atheist. That was mainly because too many Christians talk about Christianity as if it's only relevant in the next life. Listening to them I concluded it would be best to do my own thing as long as I could, and then become a Christian when I was an old man just to hedge my bets. I wanted to have my cake, AND the gusto.

Actually, I wasn't sure I even believed in the next life. My life was hell. I didn't want to become some sort of passive-aggressive wimp who never had any fun in order to maybe go to Heaven when I died.

I went to church most of my life, but I never heard one sermon on a major reason why Jesus came to earth. You may not have either. Again, Jesus said He came to earth to give us life more abundantly [1].

That's wonderful news. He didn't just come to give us pie-in-the-sky in the sweet bye and bye. He came to give us our just desserts. He came so we can have our cake and eat it too. It's what I call pie-on-the-plate religion.

He knew in order to accomplish that He would have to help us with some things. Not the least of these was sin. Sin, or what we might today call compulsive behavior, binds us.

Because I didn't know that Jesus came to give me an abundant life I didn't live the way He wanted me to. My motto as a teenager was, "live it up now you can live it down later."

I got into smoking when I was twelve, drinking in bars when I was fourteen, and sex with girls when I was sixteen. I sang in a rock band when I was seventeen. Drugs, partying, making a lot of money, and the other stuff young people do to grab all the gusto in life came later.

The problem was there was a diminishing return on my sins. I needed more and more of them to satisfy me. By the time I gave my life to Christ I felt that one woman wasn't enough, I needed six.

Drinking on weekends wouldn't do it; I wanted to party all the time. Yet the parties weren't even fun anymore, and I also could no longer control my life.

In desperation, I gave my life to the Lord, not because I wanted to go to Heaven. Jesus didn't evangelize people by asking them, "If you were hit by a chariot tonight where would you spend eternity."

He reached people by helping them with their needs. He demonstrated the healing Love of God. He's still doing that today. I gave Him my life because I just wanted some peace of mind. Fortunately, I knew some Christians who had more of that than I did, and there came a point when I wanted what they had.

Imagine my shock and delighted surprise when I learned that He would also give me all the other things I mentioned. Love, joy, meaning, true fulfillment, these are the very essence of what He wants for all of us.

Jesus teaches that sin is what enslaves us [2] and I'm living proof of that. The more sin I indulged in the more I wanted until my life was spinning out of control.

He also teaches us that He can set us free from our indentured servitude to sin. By giving us what we truly need instead of the counterfeit, by filling up our deepest emptiness with His Spirit of perfect Love, He can free us from our compulsion to self destructive behavior. When Jesus sets us free we are free indeed.

When I first surrendered to His love, I was instantly free of most of my destructive patterns. I loved everybody. I no longer wanted to use people. Even my over active sex drive was substantially tamed. When you have real love on the inside, you don't need a substitute that can never satisfy you.

I didn't crave alcohol anymore. I could drink and not even want to get drunk. God had accepted me, I no longer needed mood altering chemicals to artificially help me relax and accept myself.

I could go on and on, but you get the picture. My life was instantly, and thoroughly, different.

The problem was, I thought every problem I had was dealt with. It wasn't. Don't get me wrong, the Lord had truly set me free. His Spirit had given me the power to overcome every temptation I would ever face. But there were many I didn't want to overcome.

My soul wasn't fully restored. That will take the rest of my life [3]. And in the meantime, this spiritual cancer called sin was still lodged within me [4]. It would again try to take over my life.

This brings us to another reason why Jesus came to earth. I've already said it a couple of times. He came to bind up the broken-hearted, restore sight to the blind, and free those who had been wounded and broken by sin [5]. This is an essential part of the work Jesus came for, especially in the times which we live.

Centuries earlier, the prophet Jeremiah said that in the latter days, God Himself would heal our pain [6]. In promising this he recognized a few things. First, at the end of time, people would be given over to sinfulness like no other people in history had ever been [7].

Second, as I said earlier, *where sin abounds pain abounds*. Sin wounds us. It contains a spiritual poison, which if untreated, would destroy us. Finally, if we are to become truly free from our sin, we must be healed.

No one escapes life unscathed. One way or another we all experience a broken heart. Until it's healed, the hurts that remain within us offer Satan a foothold to use to try and take back our lives.

As I've shared in earlier chapters, the Lord promises to heal all our diseases, to save us body, soul, spirit, and to totally restore our soul. He not only promises to do it, but He has the ability to make good on the promise. He came not only to free us from the penalty of our sin but also to free us from its power.

How can He do that? Jesus lived a sinless life [8]. He's the only person who ever has. But because He has, He can give us the power to do the same.

When we receive His Spirit into our life and give Him control of us, we receive the same power of the Holy Spirit that enabled Him to live a sinless life [9]. It's as if we have this fatal disease called sin. If we don't get the antidote we will die.

Jesus has the antidote. When we receive Him, we also get the antidote. We receive the power we need not only to heal our pain but also to keep us from doing the things that cause it.

It gets even better. He can also conquer death. You see, sin was the penalty for death [10]. Unchecked, sin inevitably causes death. But when Jesus came to earth and lived a sinless life He broke its power over mankind.

Because He lived a sinless life those who receive Him have the same power to gradually, little by little, overcome the sin that would otherwise destroy them too.

Another way of saying this is that because He made it to Heaven we can too. And that's the best news of all.

Heaven is a wonderful place. There's no suffering or selfishness there, nothing contrary to God's Love.

There's no lack, no hardship, no disharmony and strife. It's the Garden of Eden, a true utopia, only better, because it can never be polluted with Satan's lies and deceits.

And it all begins when we come to know the Lord [11]. In Him, we have an inexhaustible source of grace, mercy, and unconditional love. In Him we have someone who knows everything that made us the way we are and what it will take to undo the damage that's been done.

In Him, we have the One who has the power to heal us inside and out, and to free us from all that would keep us from getting the love and spiritual resources we need to have the very best that life has to offer [12].

God is not a perfectionist; He's a perfect Father. He doesn't need us to be good so He can look good, He is good.

And that's quite a difference. His eternal paternity more than compensates for all the inadequacies of our past. He's not only the highest power there is on earth and in Heaven but thankfully, He's benevolent.

The One who holds the reigns of the universe is the very essence of perfect Love. He not only loves you, He genuinely likes you.

So that's why I believe that if you need healing, Jesus should be your Higher Power. He's not only the highest Power there is, but He's also the best news I've ever encountered.

If you want to find out for yourself, it's as simple as asking Him to forgive you for living your own life and going your own way. If you're ready to let Him call the shots, simply say, "Father forgive me, Jesus come into my life, I give it to you. Thank you."

If you're not ready for that yet you can still do something. You can give as much as you can to as much of God as you understand. Ask God to show you He's as good as I say.

Then look for some real Christians, people who are filled with the love of God, committed to the Bible as His dependable Word, and willing to share with you and answer your questions. Spend some time with them and ask them all your questions, and make sure they show you the answers in the Bible. It's the only dependable source of authentic truth that I know.

If you've given your life to Him you will need to find a biblical church where you can worship, learn, grow, and progress on your healing journey.

We are developing a network of like minded churches. If you'd like your church to be trained to do this kind of healing ministry, contact us. We'll be glad to help.

In the meantime, if you visit www.SoulDr.com, there you will find a list of tapes, healing retreats and seminars we have available to help you. You may call us to order them or get more information.

God Bless you! I pray that your healing will continue to spring forth speedily, and that you will soon know the joy of real freedom in Christ if you don't already.

If you do know it, I pray you'll find more of the healing He has for you. Nothing else has done more to improve every facet of my life. I sincerely hope and pray that for you, as well.

SCRIPTURE TO MEDITATE ON THIS WEEK:

"But as many as received Him, to them He gave the right to become children of God, to those who believe in His name: who were born, not of blood, nor of the will of the flesh, nor of the will of man, but of God." (John 1:12-13)

FOOTNOTES:

[1] John 10:10

[2] John 8:31-36

[3] Philippians 1:6

[4] Romans 7:20

[5] Luke 4:18

[6] Jeremiah 30:17

[7] II Peter 3, Matthew 24

[8] Hebrews 4:15

[9] John 1:12

[10] Genesis 2:7

[11] John 17:3

[12] Isaiah 1:19-20

THE MOST IMPORTANT QUESTIONS IN ALL OF LIFE:

1. Have you asked Jesus into your life?

_____

_____

_____

2. Have you given Him control, allowing Him not just to be Lord of the whole earth, but also Lord of your life?

_____

_____

_____

3. If not, and if you're ready to, you may do so simply by praying, *"Lord, forgive me for my sins. Come into my life. I give it to you. Thank you. In Jesus' name."*

4. If you've not done that but are ready to know Him better you may pray: *"Lord, I give as much as I can to as much of you as I understand. Help me know that you are truly the best way for me to live. In Jesus' name, Thank you."*

Remember He said, "If you seek for Him with all your heart you will find Him." And if you find Him, you will find the only One who can heal all your diseases and free you from all your captivities. Better yet, you'll find the One who can show you the best way to get the most out of this life and Heaven.

CHAPTER 17

VITAMINS, NUTRITION, AND EMOTIONAL HEALTH

I WOULD BE REMISS IF I DID not include a section on the landmark work being done with vitamin and nutritional therapy to treat, and often cure, symptoms of emotional disease.

I long ago discovered that simple things, like St. John's Wart, can be quite effective in inexpensively treating depression. It causes virtually none of the side effects and hazards posed by drugs, which often just mask the symptoms of deeper pathological issues.

I also take Vitamin C and E regularly to keep me healthy, and feel much better all the time. I rarely get sick, and when I do it doesn't last long. Simple garlic pills help keep my allergy symptoms at bay, and Vitamin A has helped me keep my skin tone, and made me able to live in Southern California without fear of melanoma.

Lysine helped to lower my cholesterol substantially. Yet for all of this, I'm admittedly novice in my knowledge about all that vitamins and minerals can do for our physical and emotional well-being.

No one can deny the emotional benefits of feeling good and staying healthy are enormous. When we feel good physically, it greatly affects our emotionally state. But there are people who are going way beyond this. They are treating severe emotional states as well.

I began learning about this from a letter which a friend forwarded to me. It was written by a young man who was healed of schizophrenia through nutritional therapy. His name is John Hammell and he's now leading the fight to keep vitamins, minerals, and nutritional therapy easily accessible and inexpensive. [1] In a lengthy phone conversation he made me aware of the work of others who are seeing dramatic results in treating emotionally based diseases with nutrition and vitamins.

I also spoke with Alice Ortugar, a helpful employee at the Well Mind Association of Greater Washington [2]. From her I learned about Abram Hoffer, whose work dealing with Orthomolecular Treatment, or the chemical roots of emotional illnesses, has helped many thousands [3].

While I've been told that Vitamins B3, B6, and E can reverse the symptoms of schizophrenia, they shouldn't be taken without consultation to determine the appropriate dosage. Blood sugar, thyroid, and exposure to the multitude of toxins omnipresent in our society can all cause symptoms of emotional disease.

The Carl Pfeiffer Treatment Center in Naperville, Illinois [4] analyzes a person's chemical makeup to determine the correct mental and elemental nutrients necessary to correct imbalances and restore mental and emotional health.

Julian Whitaker's newsletter contains valuable information on a full range of nutritional health issues [5]. In *Wrong Diagnosis, Wrong Treatment: The Plight of Alcoholics in America*, Dr. Beasley shows that many alcoholics are hypoglycemic [6].

Very simply put, they crave sugar, and that's the key ingredient in alcohol. I'm told that the famous Bill W, who started Alcoholics Anonymous, recognized the importance of Orthomolecular Treatment to address the chemical imbalances that rendered people vulnerable to alcoholism.

Allegedly, members of his board overruled him in making such knowledge integral to their treatment regimen, probably keeping untold millions of people bound to a debilitating fight for control of their lives.

There are powerful people behind the American Medical Association and pharmaceutical companies that don't want you to have this information. Literally billions are at stake in selling their often debilitating and inadequate prescriptions.

And while we would think that the FDA is assuring us that the drugs we take are proven safe and effective, in fact the FDA has in many people's mind's become the tool of the pharmaceutical industry. There are known incestuous relationships between the drug companies and the governing board of the FDA.

Do your own research on these issues. It's your health. The following books can point you in the right direction, getting you up to speed on the people and treatments that are going beyond treating symptoms and getting to the real roots of emotional disorders.

FOOTNOTES:

[1] Contact John C. Hammell, International Advocates for Health Freedom, 2411 Monroe Street, Hollywood, FL. 33020. Phone 1-800-333-2553, or fax (954) 929-0507. You may access his web site at www.iahf.com, and email him personally at jhamiahf.com.

[2] Well Mind Association of Greater Washington. You may call them at (301) 949-8282.

[3] Hoffer's work includes *Smart Nutrients*, with him and Walker, and *Putting it all Together: The New Ortho-molecular Medicine*, among others.

[4] See. *Nutrition and Mental Illness*, by Carl Pfeiffer.

[5] Contact Julian Whitaker at, The Whitaker Wellness Institute, 1-800-SURGEON.

[6] See, *Wrong Diagnosis, Wrong Treatment: The Plight of Alcoholics in America*, by Dr. Joseph D. Beasley.

Other books to check out: *The Way Up from Down*, by Dr. Priscilla Slagle, and *A Dose of Sanity*, by Sydney Walker, and *Food, Teens, and Behavior*, by Barbara Reed and *Natural Cures*, by Kevin Trudeau.

ADDENDUM I

PEACE WITHOUT PROZAC: SEVEN STEPS OUT OF DEPRESSION AND ANXIETY

HERE ARE SOME SIMPLE THINGS you can do to help you find perfect peace in almost any situation. Every client I've recommended this to has loved it.

1. Take a hike! Walking is powerful. Thoreau once said he never had a problem that didn't go away after a long walk. It's almost miraculous. Since I've been walking out my problems I've experienced a peace and freedom I never believed possible, even during the most trying times.

2. Journal: For me, journaling is like writing a letter to God. Some call journals the paper psychiatrist. Journaling gets the problem out of your hands and into more competent ones.

3. Gratitude: Many people recommend gratitude as a potent weapon in your arsenal against anxiety and depression.

First thing in the morning think of five things you're grateful for. Write them down. It will change the tenor of your whole day.

4. Annihilate anxiety: Anxiety is the key thing that causes depression. The Bible's injunction to 'be anxious in nothing' is great counsel. Anxiety never helps it only hurts. Resist the temptation to catastrophize and think instead of good potential outcomes, or merely think of something else. You'll feel peace seep back into your soul.

5. Retread your head: I've retreaded my own head and taught others in my Spiritual Mentoring group to do the same. This means replacing negative, self defeating attitudes with positive life enhancing ones. The Bible is alive and powerful. If you believe in it, find scriptures that promise what you desire, personalize them and meditate on them daily. If you don't believe in the Bible use affirmations based on truths you do believe.

6. Supplication: This fine old word simply means to humbly request what's best and leave the outcome to God. New studies show not only that prayer makes things better, but also that the most effective prayers are prayers of relinquishment. Just make a request then trust God for His best outcome.

7. Start a Transformational Healing Group: Find two or three friends who would benefit from *The Ultimate Breakthrough* and start your own healing group. Everyone I know who has done this has helped themselves and others find healing.

Finally, remember something my blind mother used to tell me when things were really bad: "Everything will work out, it always does!"

Contact us at www.SoulDr.com for an exciting nurturing free E-zine on Spiritual Growth and Healing. It also offers you discounts on our upcoming retreats, seminars and products to assist you in your personal growth and healing.

You probably know many friends and loved ones with whom you would like to share *Peace Without Prozac*. You can get quantity discounts as well as our other EBooks, and CD and DVD series on *Transformational Healing, Improving Your Emotional IQ* and *Precious Pearls – Spiritual Wisdom for an Abundant Life*.

All this is available at www.SoulDr.com

ADDENDUM II

SOFT INTERVENTION

S O IT ALL COMES DOWN to this question: how do we provide peace without Prozac? How can we better help people find total freedom from the bondage of alcoholism and drug addiction, and liberate them from sexual addiction, over eating, work addiction and now even addiction to computer games, smart phones and other devices?

Sacred Psychology provides real answers. Wonderful Counselors need to know what to do. Transformational Healers must offer real healing so that transformation does not become just talk.

When I was appointed as the holistic counselor to our county drug and treatment coalition I was stunned to learn about the magnitude of the drug problems we face as a nation. One city in our county had a 78% increase in drug arrests in one year. A small but growing percentage of young men who take marijuana will become psychotic but they don't tell you that when they try to convince you that the state should make money on it by legalizing it. Over 50% of new psychiatric diagnoses in my county result from marijuana. Legalized medical marijuana can help certain medical conditions dramatically but legitimizing it recreationally causes problems we don't even want to think about. One state that did this had a 100% increase in car accidents caused by marijuana. In one US city, 60% of DUIs are from heroine. In that state almost 40 people per 100,000 are overdosing.

Our war on drugs has failed miserably. A drug expert told me that ISIS and al-Qaeda are flooding the US with drugs in order to further destroy us from within. And it's working. The real cause of military suicides? Not PTSD. Over 70% have not even been in combat. According to the documentary film The Hidden Enemy over 60% of our active military take prescription drugs given to them by the military and 90% of their children do.

Many other issues related to both prescriptions and illicit drugs are equally shocking. I learned that when people can't get prescription drugs to kill their pain or when they become too expensive they often turn to heroin or synthetic drugs. Some of these synthetic drugs are so toxic that DEA agents must use hazmat suits when handling them. If they sweat while touching a pill, the chemical can get into their skin and kill them instantly. And these pills are designed to look like ordinary prescription meds.

Overdoses from prescriptions and illicit drugs are becoming epidemic in our whole society. I met mothers whose children had overdosed and died. They began training police departments and other medical professionals to use new drugs that can immediately stop an overdose and save a life. But as demand increased the cost of those drugs soared from $250 to $4,500 per dose! Where are the FDA and our legislature when we need their protection? Sometimes it seems as if the fox is guarding the hen house.

It soon became obvious to me that we needed to develop new ways to get people off of drugs and help them find freedom. Hundreds of thousands of people are afflicted with debilitating and destructive behaviors related to both illicit and prescription drug abuse. Every year tens of thousands die and almost as many take their own lives. Millions of beloved friends and family members suffer when we fail to provide compelling, consistent and competent care and yes, even cure.

These people have stubborn difficult perplexing problems. Someone once said that for every complicated problem there is a simple answer that's wrong. Perhaps this is truer in the areas of compulsion and addiction treatment than in any other issue related to health. Our solutions must be totally holistic if they are to heal and save lives. Sadly, anything less has way too often proven to be inadequate at best.

Professional Intervention, where addicts are confronted and forced to enter treatment, is usually hard and expensive. More often than not it fails. As a wounded healer, I've sometimes seen miracles free people from alcoholism, drug addiction and overeating in one session. But for most people, the perilous journey to freedom entails a far longer and more precarious path. That's where we need a new Paradigm for treatment that I call the Soft Intervention.

The problems with traditional intervention and treatment are manifold. First, the person being confronted with a forced intervention may not have hit bottom yet. He or she may much prefer their addiction to the harshness of life without pain killers and devoid of the artificial succor of their familiar comfort. Usually intervention is commissioned by family members and friends who have bottomed out. That doesn't mean the addict is ready. I've often said that I can help anyone who wants it and no one who doesn't. This is probably truer with addiction than any other self-destructive problem.

Another huge issue is the vast unspoken problem of the manifold failures of traditional treatment programs. Hard data is not easy to come by, but as near as we can tell, they fail approximately 70% of the time. And both traditional intervention and traditional treatment are extremely expensive. Intervention can cost a thousand dollars a day and take two or three days. Treatment costs an average of $900 a day and requires at least 30 days. If it's going to fail 70% of the time the person will need at least three times for it to succeed and just the financial cost is huge. Some Cadillac treatment centers cost $100,000 for a month. A friend in the local drug and treatment coalition told me of a woman who went 16 times at $100,000 a month until she ran out of money and was out on the streets.

Soft Intervention is potentially much more successful and far less expensive for many reasons. When I do a Soft Intervention, apart from any coercion, the person must be able to tell me that they are sick and tired of being sick and tired and they will do anything to get the help they need. So first of all, no one is forcing them to do this; it's their own choice. That factor alone makes the battle far easier and success much more likely.

Secondly, they don't need to spend money for the intervention. Instead, far less money is spent on intensive upfront sessions so we can get to the root of their problem and begin to solve it comprehensively. In a recent example, a client flew in to see me from another city. We had seven hours of sessions spread out over a day and a half and when she returned home I was convinced that she would finally succeed and conquer her addiction. So was she.

Why was she so confident? First of all she had tried treatment on three previous occasions and had joined 12 step groups and sought traditional counseling over many years. She knew what didn't work. I offered her options that she believed would work. And it's a law of faith that whatever we sincerely believe, good or bad, always happens.

One more reason traditional addiction treatment and counseling fails is because it's focused on the erroneous belief that the person has a disease; one that can never be cured. They have a dis-ease, but that's very different from a disease.

Another reason traditional methods fail is because the primary focus is on helping the person quit their addiction. While it would seem logical that this should be their main motivation, if you know anything about the power of belief and disbelief and what lots of people call the law of attraction, you know that you receive whatever you focus on. If the primary focus is on overeating, you are going to crave food more than you ever did before. This is what the Bible calls the downward spiral of "the law of sin and death." This is why the Apostle Paul's statement in Romans six is so powerful. He said sin will not have dominion over us because we are not under law but under grace. In I Corinthians 15 he said "The strength of sin is the law." What does that mean? If I say to you right now, "Whatever you do, do not think of a red-faced monkey," you will probably immediately see a red-faced monkey for the first time in your entire life. That's human nature; it's how our congenital rebellion reacts to law. Original sin is a reality whether you believe in it or not.

This is precisely why the Bible cautions us that whenever we teach God's Word we must make sure that it ministers grace to the hearers. It's easy to guilt people; lots of preachers do it in every sermon, but that doesn't help them change. It makes it more likely that they will not be able to change. Grace not only saves us from the penalty of sin, it's the only thing that can save us from its power. This is why 'shoulding' on people and shaming them is the worst possible way to help them. Forced legalism virtually destroys our capacity to obey. This is why perfectionism is literally a killer.

Contrary to popular religious beliefs, God is not a perfectionist, He's a perfect Father. He doesn't need us to be good so He looks good, He is good. The reason He wants us to be good is because it's in our own best interests. Virtue truly is its own reward.

He loves us broken sinners but He loves us too much to leave us that way.

So grace is our only way out. It's the only path that leads to true and lasting liberty. Grace is not a prescription for licentious living, it's actually the only key to unlocking our chains. It "breaks the power of canceled sin and sets the captives free."

If I tell you that you have a disease and you must immediately quit feeding it and never again give into it for the rest of your life I am intensifying the pressure. You will feel an even greater need to indulge your temptation. I realize this is controversial and runs smack dab in the face of traditional addiction treatment and counseling but that tradition isn't working. It's failing because we are violating everything we instinctively know about human nature.

I've said before that the overeater must eat every day and the married sex addict must have sexual relationships. They must learn how to treat food as food and sex as sex. Obviously you can't say to them they can never eat again or have sex again without starving them or their marriage to death.

The practical applications they need in order to cope are similar to other addictions. What if some people can heal their core pain sufficiently so that they can eat, drink and have sex without abusing them? Concerning alcohol, this may well be possible for some but not for others. I know I can never smoke a cigarette again, I'd be instantly hooked. But another person, after healing their core pain and rounding out their life may be able to enjoy a cigar or a glass of wine and never again have it control them.

Another example is: work addiction. It is every bit as powerful an addiction as food and sex. It can be even more compelling because we don't emulate the food or sex addict like we do the work addict. Work addiction is what I call the 'Acceptable Addiction.' We don't complement the alcoholic or food addict for their incredible ability to consume but we often praise the work addict for his wonderful work ethic. And yet the children of the work addict will manifest the same symptoms as the children of an alcoholic.

Another new addiction that is being recognized is being called Digital Heroine: addiction to devices like smart phones, Play Stations and other entertaining devices. Addiction experts see the same changes in brain chemistry when the use and abuse of these things becomes uncontrollable.

So if grace is the only way to break the dominion of sin over our lives we need to consider different ways to relate to the drug or alcohol addict. What if instead of calling it a disease and telling them they must never ever do it again or they will die, we say to them, "You may revert but it's not the end of the world. I will still love you; God will still love you, the people who really matter will still love you and we will help you conquer this no matter what it takes." Grace coupled with Tough Unconditional Love defuses the tenacious power of the law of sin and death and disrupts the downward spiral of compulsion and self-destructive behavior. It's why Jesus is better at saving us from our sins than any other power known to man. In fact he was named Jesus because he would save us from our sins and grace is his primary method of operation.

This too bears repeating: grace doesn't just save us from the penalty of our sin; it also rescues us from the power of our sins.

Fundamentalist denominations that forget this and create strict barriers against any use of alcohol create more alcoholics than almost any other religion or belief system. Maybe that's why Jesus' first manifestation of His glory was by turning 88 gallons of water into wine at a wedding when people had already had a lot to drink. And it was wine, folks, not Welches! Religious leaders and groups that obsess about sex cause similar problems. Billy Graham was once told by the president of a major hotel chain that they sell more in room pornography when there are pastors' conventions than at any other time.

The same is true for religious groups that enforce extreme condemnation for sexual sins. The state that does this most, Utah, also has the biggest problem with porn addiction in the entire nation. We may eventually find it also has other hidden sexual problems as well. Courageous authors have recently forced their issues with incest to the surface. We only have to look at the Catholic Church to see the damage that unbiblical and unrealistic suppression of legitimate sexual needs and relationships has done to their clergy, thousands of children and their entire religion.

The real Jesus, the Jesus of the gospels and the Apostle Paul, is the addicts' best hope. He alone offers us saving grace and genuine freedom from eminent self-destruction through the practical palpable power of the Holy Spirit. Again, hard numbers are difficult to find but it appears that Christian treatment programs are successful more than 80% of the time (contrasted with an apparent 70% failure rate of secular programs) and yet most traditional treatments and rehab strictly forbid any overt mention of Jesus Christ. Is it any wonder they fail?

In addition to starting from a place of grace, a Soft Intervention does a few other things differently as well.

First of all, not only do I not tell my client they have an incurable disease, I share with them my belief that when a person heals their pain they no longer need aspirin, no matter what aspirin they use.

I offer them the very real hope of healing the pain that fuels their self-destructive behavior. I've obviously spoken about this already in this book and shown people the steps and methods they misused to heal their pain but I can't begin to tell you how encouraged addicts are when they learn that they can heal the underlying cause of their dis-ease.

Healing probably won't occur in the initial sessions of a Soft Intervention but it can happen very efficiently at a healing retreat or seminar that costs a fraction of the price of a week's worth of treatment. The weekend retreats cost about $1000 and seminars cost as little as $197. Those can be used at a later time to heal the core primal pain and give the patient the opportunity for a quantum leap forward in their healing journey.

Another thing that I do differently in a Soft Intervention is that I treat the problem far more holistically. In the initial sessions, I seek to determine what the person's daily life is like and whether they have anything to live for. Most people don't. So I return to the idea that addiction is a consequence of doing that which is not your passion. Then together we try to find out what the person's heart's desire really is. This may take a while but at least we start the process. I do that with this simple question: if you could do anything you wanted and money was not an object and you knew you wouldn't fail what would you do? I ask the client to live with that question until they have a satisfying answer.

I then work with them to help them come up with a life Mission Statement, one or two sentences that define their raison d'être: their reason for being. Next, I help them discern their Vision Statement. This is a more comprehensive document that may take a full page to write. In it the person explains the type of work they would like to do, the kind of place they would like to live and the fun things they would like to experience in their life including the people they would like to surround themselves with and the toxic people they need to exclude.

One other especially maddening thing about traditional rehab and treatment is its perpetual dependence on 'medicine men.' Because of its roots in a medical model for treatment, they get people off of hard drugs and then if they have trouble with sleeping, anxiety, depression or other emotionally based issues they get them hooked all over again on prescription drugs. Since they have no true healing modality they usually tell them they must take those drugs for the rest of their life! The legalized pushers strike yet again, swapping one compulsion for a supposedly less harmful one. One way or another, the doctors usually win with this model and sadly the patient almost always loses. We are creating a nation of zombies. The walking dead are all around us; you can see it in their eyes.

This has no semblance whatsoever to the abundant life Jesus said he came to give us. I know this first hand; it's why I feel so strongly about it. When I was 22, I was addicted to prescription drugs. They made my life a living hell. I got so depressed I slept 18 hours a day to avoid reality. My doctor was clueless and just renewed my script whenever I had an appointment. It pushed me to the precipice of suicide.

As I gazed over the lip of the abyss, convinced that there was no way out, I decided to buy a gun the next morning and end it. As I reached to turn out the lamp I noticed the old King James Bible on my night stand. My grandmother had given it to me when I was 10 after my grandfather died. She apparently found comfort in it. I found nothing but gobble dee gook. Many times over the years I tried to read it, every time I failed. It was an archaic, incomprehensible tome to me. By then I had become an atheist. But for some reason I picked it up one last time. "God," I said, "If you're there, I need you to speak to me." I realized I'd tried everything I knew that I was willing to try to find happiness and failed miserably; nothing worked. The only thing I hadn't tried was God on His terms and I had no idea what they were.

I started at the beginning of the New Testament, reading just the words of Jesus which were in red. To my chagrin, I really liked Him. He loved sinners and didn't get along with religious people. He had no worries about money; when He needed it He pulled coins from the mouth of a fish. He hung out with sinners. He turned water into wine at a wedding – a lot of wine, and the people were already half looped. That was His first miracle! Unlike me, He never worried about money or clothes or what people thought of Him. He also didn't mince words. Though He was eminently kind and compassionate, He told it like it is. I liked Him a lot.

By the time I got half way through the Sermon on the Mount I realized I was a sinner. He didn't say that, I just knew it. When I compared myself to Christians I wasn't half bad but compared to him I was nobody. I had done my own thing since I was 12 and big enough so my father couldn't push me around anymore. I had messed up my own life. I had no one to blame. No one but Me! I remembered Billy Graham - the same guy I used to mock when I saw him on TV – say that we needed to invite Jesus into our heart.

Three days earlier I had stopped taking the damn drugs. At first I felt almost normal again but my symptoms came creeping back in. You see, I'd become psychotic from doing pot. A small number of young men do have that reaction. That's why I was taking prescription drugs; they were antipsychotics. I'd been told I'd need them for the rest of my life. After two days without them I started feeling like a normal human being again. But soon my delusions came creeping back in, compounded by tremors from the withdrawal. That's why I was so intent on ending it all. My whole life was truly hellacious.

I climbed out of bed and knelt before that Bible. I thought of all the people I'd hurt, running roughshod over them in my reckless and feckless pursuit of pleasure. "Father, forgive me," I pleaded. "Jesus come into my life, I give it to you."

Then it happened.

A warm, wonderful, incredibly gentle, yet powerful spiritual lightning bolt from heaven hit my heart, flooding it to overflowing with palpable love, total acceptance, deep tranquility and bliss. And most surprising of all: I was instantaneously healed. My shaking stopped immediately, my delusions evaporated. In one deliciously cogent moment, all of life made sense. I finally found what I'd been searching for, what everyone sought: unspeakable love, delectable joy and a deep abiding peace that transcends understanding and trumps all rational comprehension. And I discovered so much more: clarity. In an instant my life morphed from a dismal black and white and the most tepid tedious grey to the brightest most brilliant and vibrant living color I could ever imagine.

This is what the secular world desperately tries to keep hurting people away from. And you say you don't believe in Satan? This indescribably delectable 'born again' experience is what we replace with chemicals. This awesome new life is what the world tries to sell us their sorry sad substitutes for like new cars, fancy clothes, and makeovers – you know, all that deep transcendental meaningful stuff!

What I stumbled onto was exactly what Satan desperately wants to prevent us from ever discovering: a God of unflinching love, infinite power, intense compassion and yes, omnipotent healing. This is why I abhor the abuse of prescription drugs; it's why I believe most secular treatment is doomed to fail. Leave out Jesus and there's just not enough juice to get the whole job done.

My last in person session with the client I mentioned earlier left her with a self-generated 10 point plan to achieve the goals she had for her new life. I later found out that on the first day she returned home she tackled the toughest action. This is exactly what I encouraged her to do; attack the hardest things first. By day three she had started working on the first five items on her list, including things like getting the toxic people out of her life and finding ways to eat healthier. Her plan also incorporated confronting habitual patterns of escape like watching too much television and falling asleep on the couch. Most importantly, it focused on finding ways to do the positive things she really enjoyed and always wanted to do.

Within less than three weeks of seeing her for the first time she had found a new place to live that she really liked and was making plans to move there. It's near a church that has a children's nursery where she can volunteer and just perhaps discover her reason for being.

I asked her for written permission to help her assemble a personal support system. She readily agreed to allow me to speak with three other people in her life who could help her with various aspects of her plan. All three of those people volunteered to be available to help her in numerous capacities, one with financial responsibility, another health and accountability, the third as an ardent cheerleader. Each of these people also derived deep personal satisfaction from helping her.

Her aching loneliness was now a thing of the past.

Another facet of being a Wonderful holistic Transformational Counselor is helping people find naturopathic solutions to their health issues. These are readily available on the Internet today.

She next committed to seek out a local Christian-based recovery network and another person in her support system and I committed ourselves to being available 24/7 if she needed us in the interim. We would be a stopgap for her that was just a phone call away until she found a suitable and compatible sponsor for her sobriety. I also told her I wanted a weekly teleconference with her until she got the other pieces in place and felt that she didn't need to speak with me that often. As she gets stronger we will talk every other week and eventually every third week and eventually once a month. This and her volunteer support system will carry her through until she has the other necessary pieces in place to be able to do without us.

As soon as it's convenient she will attend a healing seminar or retreat to address her core primal pain and heal it. I believe that a year from now her life will be totally different. She actually looked like a new person when she left my office to return home. But she and her friends and family and I are all convinced that this time she will conquer her compulsions and become a happy, healthy and joyfully contributing member of society. And all of this is done for a full year at a fraction of the cost of one month's treatment.

At TIP we are training an army of Certified Transformational Counselors who can offer Soft Interventions to the hundreds of thousands of people who so desperately need them. For info, go to www.SoulDr.com – you'll be glad you did.

ADDENDUM

HIM-POSSIBLE

AT SOME POINT, I DEVELOPED A reputation for being a counselor to whom other professionals sent their impossible cases. I've always believed that what is impossible for man is HIM-Possible for God. But honestly, I recently wondered if that were really true so I thought back to some of the impossible cases that I'd worked with. I was shocked to discover that there were over 40 people who fit into that category. This included a housewife who had been programmed to forget that she was a victim of Satanic Ritual Abuse. Then there was the Catholic nun who had been in therapy for 10 years and owed her current counselor over $8000. Both of these women were freed from their issues in just three sessions. There was also the truck driver who had been raped as a young teenager and became a child molester; another man discovered that he was a botched abortion; a woman at a retreat began to become psychotic and was drawn back into normalcy in just 30 minutes. Somehow god was able to help all these people transform their lives through my work

Another woman had 21 personalities and was able to integrate them all into one whole personality in just three days at a retreat.

There was a high school principal who was a voyeur and the leader of a biker gang who was imprisoned because he was "too mean to die." Then there was the 13-year-old pyromaniac who was in and out of an adolescent psych hospital for seven years. When he was released the doctor said he never expected to have to see him again. I can never forget the hard core skeptic when I led a healing seminar at a men's prison who proclaimed us to be the real deal after one short session or the woman who had no memories before the age of 14. In three sessions she realized she had been molested by her own father for 11 years and she was well on her way to healing after just those three sessions.

Then there was the woman who had TMJ for many years and was healed in one session at a Transformational Healing Retreat. A gay man came to me because of his Agoraphobia and concluded that he really wasn't gay after all without any prompting from me. There was the lesbian who asked me to help her change her sexual orientation. In a few sessions she joyfully hugged me and said our haling work had completely changed and she later said she developed romantic relationships with men for the first time in her life.

I'll also never forget the Hawaiian woman at one of my retreats. During her healing session, she began to spontaneously name and cast out ancestral demons that entered her as a child when she was sexually abused during religious rituals. With a little help and guidance she was able to peacefully exorcise herself from the power of 29 demons to the amazement of all of us. Then there was the woman who struggled with seizures for 50 years and was healed in one session. A doctor who witnessed it stood up and testified that everything done in that session was consistent with current medical procedures in treating seizures.

An alcoholic proclaimed himself cured after one session and his pastor later told me that we'd helped him more in an hour than he had in three months of living with his family.

I remember seeing a woman healed while watching a sacred dance at one of our retreats. And how could I forget the group of rape victims and perpetrators who embraced and reconciled with each other at the end of one of our Transformational Healing Seminars?

At least 17 people have told me that I saved their life. Of course we all know that I can't save anyone from anything; in each case it was totally a God thing. I've also had the privilege of remarrying three divorced couples and being used to help many others save their marriages.

Nothing can compare to the joy of seeing hopeless people get healed. This is the calling of a Wonderful Counselor and it is our hope to help many others become Certified Transformational Counselors and so share in this unspeakable joy.

TIP INFO

K EN R. UNGER IS FOUNDER of the Transformation Incorporated Project (TIP), a training Businesses dedicated to training Churches for healing and rapid, loving organic growth (Scriptural Discipleship) and Businesses to be more humane and successful. It also equips Transformational Counselors to be more effective and efficient through Transformational Healing. It has a special component for our military called the Wounded Healer Operation (WHO).

Transformational Churches often double in size in a year or less. Transformational Businesses can save huge amounts of money by training and retaining great people, and Certified Transformational Counselors can help people more in a few sessions than years of using talk therapy, behavior modification and drugs. Through a partnership with the Charitable Giving Foundation, that has raised hundreds of millions of dollars for churches; your ministry can gain extraordinary access to funds at no cost to you. On average $1,000,000.00 is raised for every 50 people or couples who attend their free seminar.

You can earn a lucrative income by helping people through our full or part-time business opportunities. For a free 15 minute consultation, email KenRUnger@aol.com (put TIP in the subject line) or call (714) 814.3200.

Want More Information, Testimonies or Letters of Reference? Visit www.TransformationIncorporated.com or www.SoulDr. com.

CPSIA information can be obtained
at www.ICGtesting.com
Printed in the USA
FFOW01n1030080418
46160181-47346FF